Now and Then
Notes and Letters

andrewandsigridappleby

Orkney Today Limited

Now and Then Notes and Letters

by Andrew and Sigrid Appleby

Cover photograph by Gunnie Moberg

Sketches by the hand of Andrew

Published by Orkney Today Limited
1 Kiln Corner, Kirkwall, Orkney, KW15 1QX
www.orkneytoday.co.uk

Printed by NevisPrint Limited
Findhorn House, Dochfour Business Centre, Inverness

Now and Then
Notes and Letters

andrewandsigridappleby

Orkney Today Limited

To obtain further copies of
Now and Then Notes and Letters,
contact the supplier direct:

Fursbreck Pottery, Harray, Orkney, KW17 2JR
Telephone 01856 771 419

Contents

Contents (continued)

Dedicated to US.

Introduction

ow do you describe the written works of Andrew Appleby?
Quirky, eccentric, a sub-editor or proof-reader's nightmare,
ah yes ... but, above all of that, fun and highly amusing.
His monthly 'A Now and Then Note' offerings in Orkney Today
are so unique that when we asked our readers to list their favourite
and least favourite contributors, Andrew won both polls.

An acquired taste? Yes. But what a flavour.

This volume includes a 'Best of' compilations of the remedies and
reminiscences of the potter from the Parish of Harray in Orkney
– fondly known as 'The Harray Potter' – from his assessment of light
pollution, to that cure for Athlete's Foot which made so many people
squirm.

His works here are complemented, or rather stabilised, by
nourishing offerings from his long-suffering wife Sigrid, whose letters
'From France' and 'From Denmark' are also regularly published in
Orkney Today.

The couple live part of their year in France, and Sigrid's writing is
soaked in the flavour and sunshine of those special days.

My advice to all readers is just to immerse yourself in the style and
comfort of Andrew's diabolical writing, wallow in the humour and
enjoy all the excerpts of his life as they are unveiled to you. Yes, in
real life he really is like that!

Believe me, reading Andrew Appleby is a life changing experience.
Quite apart from the ten-part 'Coping With Cancer' series, which
touched so many people when it was first published, each of his tales
has a moment in it that you will find difficult to dislodge from your
memory, no matter how hard you try.

His writing has changed my life. Before I sampled it I never ate
blewits, never squirted lemon up my nose, never ate raw chive flowers
or checked out the colour of my urine after eating beetroot, an
activity highlighted in his trilogy 'Beetroot', which, incidentally, only

has two parts!

On top of that I can't listen to Pink Floyd any more without thinking of boils!

As for my favourites? Among all funeral stories, 'Shirley's Ashes' takes a lot of beating, and then there is 'Hens' ... which provides a few poignant poultry twinges from my past.

In all their offerings the characters of Andrew and Sigrid shine through. I love the road kill meals they, from time to time, provide us with, and I hope to be the one to share that last tin of snails with Sigrid.

Enjoy.

John Ross Scott
(Editor Orkney Today)

Acknowledgements

For those who I have exposed or embarrassed, portrayed or betrayed, I am truly grateful for their consent. It has been a pleasure remembering and writing all the homilies contained within this flimsy cover.

The sheer patience of the staff of 'Orkney Today,' the test readings, the emergency faxings from France, my corrections of un-corrections in 'creative spelling.' Mathew Whittles for putting this together, who has hugely influenced the style of our bijou pubicationette. George Stout who stomached the business responsibility. Monty, (Montague Ff. Chiselhunt the IIIrd) my faithful laptop, who completely understands my two-fingered approach to writing, needs congratulations, Fraser, my digital camera, so patiently supplied by Focus on Orkney, deserves praise, as does John the Editron, who flashed his piece in the murky dismals for a dark pic. Ken Amer for focussing so closely to do the flicker-pic of a potter creating Auntie's Urn. The Orkney public, who have given 'thumbs up' encouragement.

Sigrid for reading the pieces and saying "You just can't publish that!!" (So I do.) Her, also for her sheer patience. Emma of the Pottery deserves special thanks for being a part of the chickweed remedy, as does Sally Linklater, who keeps that cutting in her purse. (For she says, "It doth work".)

There are texts, which concern bowel movements!:-++++-: ! For those who have specially written to me, privately, having had relief, I wish them a 'Bog Standard Read'.

Yours, Aye Andrew.

Sigrid's P.S. ///+++/// Although I have been described as "long suffering and patient" I do enjoy a bit of mischief!!

1 Snot

'Amazingly you will find that things begin to clear up. Sometimes you might find funny little sounds and bubblings happen in your sinuses.'

Sigrid and I have recently travelled from Orkney to southern climes. On our journey we have carried memories of a superb Orkney summer. Whilst departing we saw the last swallows and the first geese.

My tiny Orkney souvenir was a little throat tickle. We sailed from Stromness on the new boat (Whatzitkalled) when a nasal itch made its presence known. I had been fighting off an Orkney cold for a week and a half – pressure of work, engagements, commitments et all, halted it. Well, when you finally relax, it happens – the cold strikes.

On the journey to our southern haven we stayed at our good friends' house in Grantham, a town famed and illustrious for being the birthplace of Maggie Thatcher whose nose gets frequently struck off her statue! There in Grantham, in bed, in Bluegate Street, at 4.04am, my nose ran, and I ran for help. I tried to speak, but vocal chords refused to issue any other sound other than a high pitched "Wheeep".

A chap with a cold and a sore throat is an 'orrible being to travel with, so Sigrid said, "Please, please take some of your own medicine." She well knows, that when others are afflicted and complain about disorders, I often suggest solutions and remedies. So, "For heaven's sake, DO!" she said. "Take it for yourself!!" What could I do? So I did.

Here it is…

For a sore throat and nasal irritation mix a solution of warm water and salt. Gargle with this allowing the liquid to trickle well down the throat. This requires skill and practise. A slow gargle – so slow that the salty water goes far below the back of your tongue. This is where a lot of infection can lie, but please don't choke or splutter.

Spit all this back of the tongue stuff out into the sink then look into the bathroom mirror and say to yourself, "I'm a better person for this."

The gargle helps the throat well, but what about the nasal tickle?

That infectious tickly sensation, of which you know will lead to greater and worser things, needs dealing with. Here's what you can do: add some more salt, pour some more hot water and when it is a comfortable temperature inhale the steam. When your nose can steep into the potion without pain, simply and slowly sniff up the briny through one nostril – left or right (I don't know the difference). At some point the warm saline stuff will stop going up. Here you sniff out hard. Then repeat nasal inhalation until the salty stuff trickles down into the top back of your throat. Sniff out hard again. It is not pleasant what you sniff out but it is far less pleasing keeping it in. When that nostril is clear, do it all over again with the other nostril.

Amazingly you will find that things begin to clear up. Sometimes you might find funny little sounds and bubblings happen in your sinuses. This is them beginning to clear. All that horrible, stored up cloggy mess in those tubes begins to shift and it may well go altogether if you repeat this private performance.

I've done the salt water bit. I didn't have the sinus problem, but I am not snoring now. The sore throat is vanquished. My nose, like Maggie's, feels nought.

Nice salty water

2 A drop in the potion

'Forced to sip he grimaced and croaked, "This is disgusting. It is the worst thing I've ever tasted!"'

If anyone tried and survived my last remedy and is willing to try another, here's a softer option, by way of reward.

This one worked a few weeks ago. Sigrid and I had been invited out for a special evening which we had been looking forward to considerably. I visited our kind host an hour before we were due there for apéritifs. I was attempting to sell him something so it was business before pleasure, but the poor chap was speechless.

"Sore throat," his friends said. "Can't utter a word."

I told him not to worry as I'd go and make him a medicine. He quickly made his escape through the back door, but I didn't know this.

I went home and gathered up the ingredients:

1. Orkney Runny Honey (Stromness)
2. Organic garlic, Wheems, South Ronaldsay
3. A lemon (foreign import)
4. Highland Park whisky, East Mainland
5. Stromness tap water – West Mainland

Method:
First get a large glass and a long spoon. Put in a good tablespoonful of honey, squeeze the lemon until pith and guts are dry and dribble it over the honey. Pour in several thimbles full of Highland Park whisky. (I lost count of the thimbles full so you can replace them with a healthy slooousch).

Put the garlic through a crusher and squash all the stuff through, this is very important. The bits that get left behind in these crushers, simply scrape out and drop in the potion: boil the water. When boiled add very slowly to your glass of goodies and stir.

As soon as the honey, whisky, garlic and lemon juice are warming and well mixed STOP adding water. Too much water is just no good at all; you're not there to quench the thirst of your patient, only to keep him alive.

Serve to sufferer immediately, if you can find him, I found him lurking in a washroom. Forced to sip he grimaced and croaked, "This is disgusting. It is the worst thing I've ever tasted."

I watched. Protests were useless; he continued to take all he could stomach. Glass handed back, I nipped out for cover.

Sigrid and I arrived late for apéritifs. Somehow we always seem to. There was our host, larger than life, laughing and chatting with guests and, naughty chap, smoking!! He said: "Whatever that filthy stuff was, it worked, but I shan't be risking a sore throat again." I didn't mention the fag, but needless to say, we had a great night.

The reasons why this mixture is beneficial is because honey is a soothing substance which is also antiseptic, it is clingy stuff and can therefore help line the throat. This is exactly why you don't want too much water. Garlic contains antiseptic substances too and its oil blends with the honey. Lemon juice bumps off a few of the older generations of germs immediately, leaving the honey and garlic to cope with the baby germs as they grow up. Highland Park is a very effective painkiller and it also fires both barrels at infections. I think it is stuff called alcohol in it that triggers these reactions off. The water, as stated before, must be used in moderation.

If you need a lasting medicine to keep in a bottle, simply omit the H2O and allow the ingredients to gruldge together overnight. You can store this in the fridge and take teaspoons full when required.

3 Hopalong Postie

*'At the Harray road end she stopped to remove the
plaster. The wound, she told me, had changed
from Post Office red to her normal hue.'*

My daughter, Ruth had met her match in Mark, so they were
getting married at Tyninghame Village Hall near North
Berwick.

Ruth wanted a grand buffet at the reception and only the best. So
– she asked Sigrid and me to do it. Without thinking of the logistics
we agreed to a cold table for 80 to 90 folk.

I won't go into the whole menu, but one of the demands was for
rolled roast, rare and well-done sirloin. Not a problem with Fletts
butcher on hand and Netta Wylie of Harray Stores for roasting. The
problem was the lashings of hot horseradish sauce Ruth and Mark
wanted to accompany the beef.

I searched many Orkney shops for proprietory pots. Yes! There
were plenty. Some stores' own brands. Mild, medium and hot,
specialists' brands, all sorts. I purchased several of the propounded
hotter ones for testing and tasting. Qualities and strength varied and
later I noticed the ingredients lists in small print. An example follows

"(First Greatest)" it read, then "Water, horseradish (36%), sugar
rapeseed oil, modified starch (maize), acetic acid, mustard flour, dried
turnip, salt, dried whole egg, flavourings, colour (Titanium Dioxide)."

It was while doing the first tastings that the mini miracle happened.
Postie arrived. My normal greeting followed "Aha! Postess with the
mostest".

"Not today," she replied and then she told me that while loading
the post van that morning she'd slipped and barked her shins. She
appealed to me, "Andrew" she winced "my shin is in agony and the
pain won't go, in fact it's getting worrrsscht. Have you got something,

please, for this pain?"

"Indeed Postritch, I have, wait there and bare thee leg, and I shall apply potion."

I nipped upstairs and took down a jar of horseradish relish and a roll of micro pore.

Postesses' wound was not open, but bruised to the bone. "Poor postie" I thought.

Then I whapped on a dollop of said condiment and spread it over the bruise. I held her foot tight so she couldn't leap while shrieking with pain.

"Patience and calm O Great Deliverer" I soothsaid to her as I applied the dressing. I then ordered "Now postie hop about on the wounded leg – Go on! Hop!" She obeyed.

"Now hop out to your van rouge and the pain will vanish in 40 minutes, then remove the plaster."

In ten minutes she'd forgotten the pain completely; though in the afternoon as she drove back to Finstown past the pottery she remembered her mid morning misery. At the Harray road end she stopped to remove the plaster. The wound, she told me, had changed from Post Office red to her normal hue.

It was a couple of days later when I did the readings of the labels and I mused "What ingredient was it that performed the cure – horseradish? Turnip? Titanium? Acetic Acid?"

I think it was the horseradish. I've never heard of a dried whole egg poltice, have you?

4 Horseradish sauce: The sequel

'The fumes and vapours erupting from the stricken root were so strong that the lid had to be replaced immediately. Our foreheads broke out in a hot sweat and our eyes ran as we slowly got over the shock.'

Having sorted through all those tiresome little jars I mentioned in 'Hopalong Postie', I concluded that the horseradish sauce within them was just not good enough for Ruth's wedding. When this happens you know that you have to make it yourself – bijou problemette – where do I get fresh horseradish in Orkney without toiling hard and grubbing it up? Answer – Wilson's, Stromness.

I enquired for their help to be rescued. A few days later, miracle, they'd sourced it from a company sooth, but I had to have 10 kilos. The cost I have forgotten but it was far less than if I'd bought sufficient in little pots or catering packs. This pleased me greatly.

The radish arrived in Stromness along with the timed deliveries of fresh and smoked goodies. Loads of scrummy stuff, and, I can tell you, we also had a gallon of Crantit Dairy double cream.

Our faithful Volvo was loaded again and I set off on the new boaty thing in Stromness which you can sleep on overnight and sail off in the morning. All perishables were in cool boxes and the sack of horseradish carefully flung in at the back. I was driving to North Berwick where I would meet Sigrid. We were to prepare the buffet in some very kind friends' house. It was fortunate indeed that they have two kitchens.

The genuine horseradish sauce needed making. We peeled two roots first. Just doing this made your eyes water and your very faces redden up. Then they needed to be shredded in the electric Mouligrinder object. "Whaaaaang," went the machine. Proud and strong roots were pulped.

Now here comes the important health and safety warning – DO NOT REMOVE LID OF MOULICHINE WITH FRAPPED UP HORSERADISH WITHOUT WEARING FACE ARMOUR.

We didn't appreciate this at the time but could have easily worked it out. When we'd unclicked the safety catch we swiftly removed the lid. We peered over the rim of the whirly chamber and our heeds were nearly blown clean off.

The fumes and vapours erupting from the stricken root were so strong that the lid had to be replaced immediately. Our foreheads broke out in a hot sweat and our eyes ran as we slowly got over the shock.

We had to calm the beast contained within the tub. Crantit double cream and pure strong vodka should do the trick (the vodka is used purely to preserve the cream). From the cool box the cream appeared, tea towels over our faces and vodka in hand we opened the whirler.

A slousch or three of Russian spirit and on top a thickness of cream covering our beaten root. That certainly cooled the fiery beast. We gave it about 33 seconds worth of whirring when you could see the blend taking place. A beautiful sight as it all folded in together. This stiffened the cream which was a good thing.

At this point Mark's Best Man, Danny, turned up. Best Man was not feeling his best at all. Indulging a little? – No – Blocked and painful sinuses. Sigrid said, "Here, Danny, Snort this." We opened the Moulilid and we all sniffed. A tamed horse indeed but still with loads of bronco spirit. "Gosh," Danny remarked. "What a potent potion."

After a few moments he asked for a tissue and blew his nose, spoke in a clear voice saying "Well! Well! Well! Golly Gee! My sinuses are clearing." A tick or two later he appealed: "Can I please have an extra whiff?" But by then that mixing was well and truly tupperwared and in the fridge.

However, we were about to harness another root. So we asked him to do the peeling. He did it serenely with eyes open and inhaling gently through his clearing airways.

His tear ducts spurted a little as the cure took effect. It was painful for him, but being the person he is, he manfully braved it.

He inhaled too, the vapours from the raw barebacked shredded stallion in the blender. We did warn him that the cure may be worse than the ailment, but he persisted. We stood clear whilst he stooped, sniffed and cleared.

The next day, the wedding day, all was ready and laid out on the tables. The marriage ceremony began in the garden of Tyninghame Village Hall. Best Man got everything right and was able to make an excellent speech. He never even faltered when he ad libbed about horseradish sauces' curative effects.

N.B. (North Berwick)
Horseradish sauce is good on beef, smoked salmon, cod salad, wounded knees and Best Man's sinuses.

Daughter Ruth on her wedding day

5 Beetroot: The Trilogy (part 1)

*'Sigrid and I enjoy the sheer delights of home-grown beetroot.
Sometimes sautéd, baked, roasted, traditionally boiled,
grated, lessered, saladified, pickled and bortched.'*

Beetroot is just one of those globes that deserves more praise
and understanding.

My grandmother was called Daisy Beartrix Appleby. We
toddlers could get our tiny tongues round Daisy, but not Beartrix, so
she was dubbed 'Daisy Beetroot' for short.

In her 92nd year I was able to phone my brother Malcolm and say
"Beetroot's dead" and then listen to the stunned pause. It was like
when, years before, I told him his Budgie, Billy Boy, had tumbled off
its mortal perch. Well, enough of these fond family reminiscences,
let's examine with relish and unrelish the delights and disappointments
of beetroot the comestible.

Just lately I have been testing store-bought products and these
beetroots were jarred or vacuum packed examples from super (non
superior) markets, and so vacuous in flavour. Also a jellied sauce
product. Flavour wise the pickled babies were poor. They seem
to have been peeled in a tumbler then boiled and vinegared. This
possible process seemed to leech what flavour there may have been
there - out.

The jellied sauce was, in my mind, too sweet and sickly.

Of three kinds of vacuumed babies, only one delivered
a 22 point three quarters percents worth of satisfaction.
Quite a low flavour factor. Apart from the taste tribunal
there was yet another disappointment – the wee factor.

This was prezactly 0.001 percent. The old norse saying
"He who pees on his socks only warms his feet once" came
true, but "He who pees red runes in the snow, hath eaten

beetroot" became quite false. No red pee, merely an unimpressive clear stream.

I spoke to my editor about this. He confesses to having eaten proprietary beetroot. I enquired of him whether there had been a rose tint at all "No! Well, not noticed" came the reply. I am sure he would have reliably informed me, after further tests, B.P. (before print) if there had been any rouge positive rizzaltz, but no!

Sigrid and I enjoy the sheer delights of home-grown beetroot. Sometimes sauted, baked, roasted, traditionally boiled, grated, lessered, saladified, pickled and borsched.

With all of these styles it is adamantly a "red letter day". If there was snow in the morning (well for me any roads) when we have guests, I now ask them to phone in a report after the morn's renal overture, because this project is getting SCIENTIFIC.

Modern society may assume that 'Emission scarlet' may mean 'HAEMORRHAGE!?' or something transmitted: poison or a hit on the epiglots by an unnoticed paint ball.

I think I can reasonably deduce now, that the non-red pee-effect is chemically induced as a marketing protection thing for our contemporary scaredy-cat planetarian colleagues. Red Pee - no sales.

Do you realise that pickled beetroots are about the hugest selling pickled products UK wise. They far outsell the humble onion, the egg, the gherkin, walnut or pickled brains.

Just imagine, with all your mind and body, if beetroot traced reddy and brains were clear, would the wally win over the onion, the ovum or walnut?

Just consider and contemplate these questions, and this other one, is the holy chemical or even saint chemical praying in our kidneys to clarify our visible liquid motions without our consent? If anyone has a clue, please speak now or forever hold thy pees.

Pee Ess It is just possible that pickled walnuts may turn into black pee. Let's find out!

6 Beetroot: The Trilogy (part 3)

*'Your beetroots progress, and as you tend them you remember
all the store bought pre-packaged ones you used to buy.
Then you wished you'd planted more, just like us.'*

If you are now pondering on when 'Beetroot - The Trilogy, Part Two' was published, ponder not. I lied! It was merely a ploy to have an exciting title and grab headlines. 'The Trilogy concentrates the mind and opens one's senses to fulfill a quest: reader, read on...'

Treated properly beetroot will never let you down.

It is also one of Sigrid's favourite crops to sow.

A drill of seeds soon shows its little green and purple sproutlings. As they grow you need to thin them out a little. This activity always saddens me when you have to abandon these helpless sparks of life, only to be dried up in the sun like stranded tadpoles on the edge of an evaporating pond. A heartless end to the brave little seedlings full of hope and yearning for maturity.

The rest of their clan, though, has room for expansion, they continue their growth and soon are nudging shoulder to shoulder again - so more pricking out. This time you can forget the sad dessication of your early "tadpoles". These slightly more formed sacrificial veggies are just edible.

Wash them under a sputring fossette, scissor off hairy tap roots,  leave the little leaves on, fling into a pan with one eighth of an inch of boiling, lightly salted water. Clap lid on and shake. Bring back to simmer for about 3 minutes 70 seconds. Then turn off heat, remove lid, chuck in a lump of butter, stir and serve on a heated plate or simply scoff straight from the pot. An unusual, interesting and tasty treat and a fine reward for that back breaking thinning chore.

Your beetroots progress, and as you tend them you remember all the store bought pre-packaged ones you used to buy. Then you wished you'd planted more, just like us. So, one pack of seeds goes effortlessly into about thriple or quadruple the amount.

Simply, take one washing up bowl, 3/4 full with dry sand or soil. Tip in the complete contents of one packet of beetroot seeds. Mix the soil or sand thoroughly until sand and seeds seem well and truly stirred.

Feed this mixture evenly into your tilthy grooves and gently water in with misty spray. The soil will moisten, the seeds will swell and they are already thinned.

After a few weeks you can forget the first thinning, knowing your "tadpoles" are going to reach at least little "froggy" size. You will be able to enjoy your first true baby beets as they biggen.

After a brief boiling their little skins slip off in your fingers, these babies, eaten warm, are a delight, and of course you will pee red. This will be a welcome sign along with appealingly rouged fingertips.

Most gardeners cast their beetroot leaves on the compost heap. My advice is "DON'T". Only discard the toughest roughest ones. Rinse the leaves and stalks, simmer them in a very little water for seven or eight minutes with lid clamped firmly on. Strain - and keep the water. Eat the leaves as you would spinach. They are wonderful, and what is more, if you have a slight "movement delay problem" this can mean the end of it. You will also feel totally good inside and renewed.

Keep the strained water in the fridge overnight and drink it first thing next morning. This certainly makes me feel very well and energised.

One summer, when Sigrid was away in France it befell me to look after and nurture her special drill of Rødbede (that's Danish you know) because she was planning borsch for September and red salads. This was the year I had discovered the delights of the leaves.

When there were enough for a goodly potfull I'd trim them off and health myself up.

All summer picking after picking, it was great.

Sigrid returned all happy and expectant. She trotted round to the back garden with her little trowel in hand only to pull up a row of gnarled, woody, shrivelled and exhausted roots. I heard a variety of Danish I'd never experienced before: this was a few years ago and we are over it now... well just.

7 A lick and a promise

*'I stuck his nose under my toes and commanded,
"Lick Boy! lick!" Robert and Audrey had never seen
this kind of behaviour before, neither had Sigrid.'*

Sigrid and I left for France early January, migrating like the birds, and will return with the swallows. It was quite amazing to us that our Volvo was not overloaded. We seemed so high above the tarmac for a change and our rear view mirror was clear to the road, not even blocked by a plant or coat sleeve, lampshade or our travelling geraniums.

We were booked on Norflynk's long voyage Hatsnot to Aberdeen. Again, we can't recall the name of the ship. It sounds to us like some gutteral choking noise. Its restaurants, bars and lounges have similar tonsil crunching combinations, and even Sigrid, who's Danish, had no truck with them. It was announced that because of the high winds it might be a bit rough. Well, it was just fine, the vessel managed very well battering through some billowing waves, but we were going to be a couple of hours late though.

At 5.30 am the tannoy man had a little joke with us. He announced that we would be overdue at Lerwick, arriving at about 9.00 am, but the breakfast restaurant and shop were open. Why wake us to tell us this? We could have slept on and found out later. A little after he corrected himself, disturbing us yet again, saying: Aberdeen at 9.00 am and we were still welcome to have an early breakfast. Sleep Vandal!!

We were going on another new shippy ferry: - the one from Rosyth to Zeebrügge. This craft departs well into the afternoon so we had plenty of time to visit friends, Audrey and Robert, in their farmhouse. There is always a welcome at Norton Mains. Not just from Robert and Audrey but also their longhaired Jack Russell Terrier, Ben. Ben gives the most amazing displays of "Hellow!! I'm here too!" He just preeks his toes and flies vertically upwards, falls down and bounces back even higher. From these levels he glees at you and everybody all at once. At last he calmed and we could be seated.

When I was comfortably arranged on the sofa, Ben just bounced onto my shoulder to lick my ears. My glasses flew off behind me somewhere. Sigrid retrieved them and cleaned them up for me. We all shouted at Ben: "STOP!! Get down!!" I pushed him off defensively and he commenced licking my hands. This is when I remembered the old adage a lady doctor confided to me, "A dog's tongue is the cleanest thing in the world, you know." Well, all that was just fine, but my hands were completely saliva'd up and Ben was lurching for my face again.

At this point I employed diversionary tackticks. I flung Ben down and smartly kicked off my shoes (not Hush Puppies, I might add), removed my socks deftly with sticky, dogspit fingers and grabbed Ben's muzzle. I stuck his nose under my toes and commanded: "Lick Boy! lick!" Robert and Audrey had never seen this kind of behaviour before, neither had Sigrid. The behaviour was mine – enjoying a doggy footbath.

Ben soon got the hang of it. His big eyes keenly met mine and he gnuzzled in. Those sore bits between the toes, where cold, sweaty skin goes white and pallid and, may I say, 'stinky,' Ben got to them first! Those festering bits whose smell often resembles that of a dead hermit crab decomposing in a groatie buckie shell (enough poetry please, Andrew). After toes, the heels: As hard as armadillo shell and just as rough. Ben's tongue's motions, rapid and skilful, softened the carapace. The toenails, "Ah!" A doggy pedicure. Like rhinoceros horn they were, until he saliva'd them, licked back the cuticles and nibbled off offending flakes of nail which had been seering into my socks.

This clever canine then did the rounds again. He'd sussed out my plates of meat alright. On his return journey over my paws, the toe interstices were plied to again. My feet had become quite desensitised from tickling, and his tongue flashed in and out, in and out, each crevice in turn. From the 'armadillo' heels, now softened to elephant hide, hard skin, which you normally scrape off after a long soak in the bath, was just being licked away and was swirling round doggie gums. A quick sole massage underneath the arches and it was toenails again.

When he finished – well, got taken off the toe-job – he looked round for other feet to do. There were none forthcoming (yet) but my feet felt better than they ever had for years. Soft skin, tingly toes and supple nails, both left and right, relaxed and warm.

We had a lovely lunch and we left for the superfast ferry. A wave to Ben and hugs from Robert and Audrey and the second leg of our journey began.

It is now several weeks later. My feet still feel brilliant and that annoying condition between the toes hath cleared up completely. I now realise that dogs of old and ancient times scavenged and still do. They scoff the most revolting, rotten, germy, disgusting things. To prevent ill to themselves and their puppies they have developed highly antiseptic saliva. This is what cured my smelly feet. Also in their special spit is a sinew-softening agent so that they can clean up dried bones. This is why my hard skin was polished off and my nails revitalised.

Footnote
We have booked another appointment (for me) with Dr Ben during our return with the swallows.

Paw Note from Sigrid
Some doggie owning friends have since come clean and concurred to us the benefits to their feet from a good licking from their K.C. Spaniels.

8 All boils over

'I soon found the gents' lav and there, poised in front of the wash basins and mirrors were genteel students, cheating by painting fangs and things on themselves, and all that tame, boring stuff.'

This tale happened nearly forty years ago. Its only relevance to Orkney is that I had visited the isles with my brother Malcolm a year or two before, and Orkney was never out of my thoughts.

Malcolm, by this time, was at the Royal College of Art studying engraving. I was at another London college doing pottery. Malcolm suggested that I went to his college's annual dance. It was called 'Suckafriend at the Horrorball'. He said I'd fit in quite well but must, however difficult, find a partner.

Topping the bill was the 'Bonzo Dog Doo Dah Band' with Vivian Stanshall and Samuel Spoons. Supporting them was an obscure group called 'Pink Floyd'. Why I recall them I don't know. I suppose it was their silly name.

Dress was extremely important. The theme of the grand fête was, after all, horror. I was informed that I had to travel 'horrible' and my date as well. So I needed to find someone with pluck.

At that time I also worked at the Peggy Foy Pottery to earn my keep (no college grant for me). I did the slip casting of children's lamps, fettling and sometimes firing. The 'girls' did the decorating and glazing in the other room.

Judith Coombes, a charming blonde, was a wow of a decoratoress, sweet seventeen and just my age. I asked her to be my 'Belle'.

At this tender age, some youths like me were prone to boils, carbuncles, cysts and acne. I will come clean here, I didn't get acne, just a great big swollen welt on my left cheek. All red and throbbing so I was already nearly half-dressed for the Ball.

17

Not surprisingly, Miss Coombes, though concerned for my pain, discomfort and well-being, announced publicly: "Well, I'm not blimping well going to any Ball with YOU looking like THAT! Horror Ball or no Horror Ball, Ok!"

I think I got the drift quite quickly, so I promised her that she could still accompany me because there would be absolutely no visible sign of imminent eruptions on my fizzog. No-one would ever suspect that her 'Beau' had this 'gem' on his cheek.

A few weeks before we had watched the 'B' horror movie 'Night of the Zombies'. This film was to be my inspiration. Judith had been studying 'Beauty Tips Weekly'. This was her inspiration.

She had decided to go all radiant, but over-the-top radiant. Well, less of that later.

I looked out my worst pair of shoes (difficult choice) and cast a large plaster left foot onto one and stuck bristles and bits of old flabby crepe bandage into it.

I found my ancient woolly mits and formed a gnarled, cup-shaped, hand with stumpy fingers for the right. (It's a question of balance, thou kens.) From the pottery wheels at college, I bagged up some sticky, wet, terracotta slurry, and a bag of drier turnings and clay dust. This was for added texture.

I then sneaked out of college back to Peggy's pottery in Kent, where Judith was getting ready in the decorators' loo. She looked 'gorgeous'. Pink and blue rinsed hair, all stuck up and back-combed, eye make-up to make a green panda jealous, luminous ears, with fingernails to match.

Judith pointed out my volcanically charged cheek and yelled, "That's it! I'm not going" I asked her: "Why not? You look so lovely and in just a few seconds you will be enchanted by your escort too. He will not let you down on your night in London Town".

I stood back and smeared a blend of clay slurry with turnings and dust all over my face, ears, neck, under my chin and into my hair.

I deftly donned my left impediment and right plastered hand saying: "Ready." Judith turned, looked and screamed.

Arm not in arm we walked to the 138 bus stop. She violently beautiful, me – just the usual. At Hayes Station I lavishly bought my belle her fare. I showed the ever-grumpy ticket collector my student pass stuck to my ghastly mit, as I limped by the barrier to our waiting carriage. He clipped her ticket and said nothing. Our train journey to town was thirty-five minutes of other passengers refusing to acknowledge us. This was strange for Judith.

At Charing Cross – walking along with other evening travellers to the bus and taxi rank – again, no-one saw us. It is funny how people are blind to the beauty around them

We entered a taxi. The driver said: "Core - blimey!! Where to? Hell and back or the graveyard again mate!"

We replied, in our most charming tones: "Royal College of Art, and the scenic route, if you please, driver".

He returned: "Might've known it. And did you two come on the train like that?"

"Yes."

"No-one say nuffink then?"

"Er, no."

"Gawd!!" He went on, "they don't know a good fing when they sees it then, do they? Aye".

We passed the illuminated Albert Memorial with London lit up to the hilt. Onward to the gaiety and excitement. Thus we arrived at the steps to the Royal College of Art.

We paid the taxi man and I attempted to hand him a tip. Instead, he said, "No mate!" as he pressed half a crown into my plaster hand.

"Eere! 'Ave a couple o' beers each on me."

"God bless you Sir!" we uttered.

"Fink nuffink ov it, mate", and he drove off into the sheer glitter of the West End.

Judith Coombes and I ascended the steps to the college's main entrance, displaying our tickets. Here we noticed that my 'make-up' was slipping a little. I needed the powder room. I soon found the gents' lav and there, poised in front of the wash basins and mirrors were genteel students, cheating by painting fangs and things on themselves, and all that tame, boring stuff.

I did the mirror bit too. I pulled my old face off and smeared on a new one in seconds flat. One pathetic changeling next to me caught my reflection in the corner of his eye. He dropped his blusher and could barely utter these, now famous words: "You – are – absolutely – horrribbble", and turned away.

"Tar", I replied.

'Pink Floyd' twinkled in the background. Drinks at the bar with the taxi man's two shillings and six pence and artistic chatter. Ian Godfrey, another potter, modelled little bronze age animals on my chin. This is when Judith and me were singled out by the college photographer and snapped for their review.

It was just like being in 'Hello Magazine'. We were applauded by Malcolm and his friends and he named me 'The Brother Grimm', but Judith's accolade was being dubbed 'Miss Katy Boyle! Starlette of the R.C.A.'s Ball 1965'

At long last 'Pink Floyd' stopped and the 'Bonzos' were announced.

Everyone rushed to the great hall and sat cross-legged on the floor facing the stage.

There was no room left for us after being delayed by the 'paparazzi'. However, I espied in the darkling gloom of the back corner of the hall, a balcony, then, concealed by a mauve curtain, a door. Miss K Boyle – Coombes – and I made for it. Her right hand in my left, we scaled the stairs behind that portal.

At the very top was an unwelcoming private club of 'elite' students. They barred our way, refusing us entry. I was then forced to circumflect and commanded: "A way through, now, please!!" They sneered. I said to them: "Do you know just who this is?" indicating Miss Coombes, "This is Miss Judith Coombes, K.B."

Then in a lower but far more stern and serious tone, "and she's prrrregnannt". They immediately ushered us past to seats where we had a fine view of the 'Dogs'. Judith said to me: "But, Andrew, I'm not pregnant". I queried her with "Well? How was I meant to know?"

The 'Bonzo Dog Doo Dah Band' was brilliant. Their classics 'Crying in the chapel', 'Intro – Outro', 'Down on Jollity Farm' and Sam Spoons playing his remarkably electric spoons. A really magical occasion.

During the 'Doo Dah's' performance these other students began picking at my 'face', then rolling up clayey pellets and buzzing them at the 'Dogs' below. I was appalled. However, they continued. Left side was used as ammo, then the right cheek became their arsenal. This was rolled up and fired Dogwards (absolute hooligans).

As they buzzed the 'Bonzos', Judith, observant as ever, spotted my cheek. She said, "It's all gone". I remarked: "No, there's still plenty left in my hair".

"No! Not clay, Andrew, your carbuncle. Or rather it's not your carbuncle. It's vanished!!"

I felt my cheek, sure enough not a trace left. Smooth skin. All boils over. Inflammation cleared and healed. No pain no more.

We left the dance, digit in digit and made back for Kent. I realised then, that by chance, I had made my very first ever clay poultice. A spot-on cure for a cheek so pure.

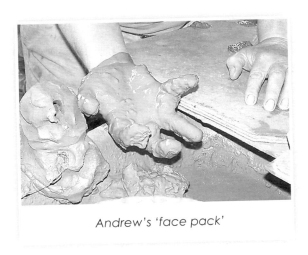

Andrew's 'face pack'

9 *The unsickening of oysters*

'The knife is then twisted mercilessly to force upper shell from lower, revealing the delicious incumbent reclining in its now semi-detached residence.'

I was four years old when my father had a wee fish van. He drove it early on a Friday to Billingsgate Market, just 3 yards 10 3/4" north of the Thames. On one of the those Fridays I awoke with the chirping of the sparrows and caught him disappearing vanwards at 04.32am. This was one of those precious, late spring mornings when the birdsong was so crisp and joyous in our pine tree. He returned to the kitchen because he'd forgotten his bakky. I caught him.

"Dad," I appealed, "Please, please take me with you."

"No, 'Nenny', you're far too young yet!"

"No, I'm not, I'm up aren't I?"

"Oh" Alright," he yawned, "but it's your own fault."

How I endear those words now: "But it's your own fault"!! The mistakes I've made.

I hath digressed – pardon.

At 05.28 we were at Billingsgate. I tugged along behind and viewed plaice and dabs, mackerel, turbot, sprats, crabs, mussels and cod. Everything from the fishy deeps and shallows was displayed there. I touched eels as they wriggled and writhed in their barrels.

Dad bought flat fish, straight fish, black fish, white fish, long fish and frightful fish, and lastly a box of Whitstable Oysters. His deal was done and brown ten bob notes were exchanged from scaley hands.

I was then lifted up in a great fish basket, weighed on a steelyard and transported in another basket on a fishporter's head for auction. '2 bob – 2/9d – 3 bob – 3/2d – a stone.' I can't exactly mind on the fetching price, but I loved the view over the basketry Whicker's World's Horizon. Sadly I didn't reach a reserve price and had to remain in poverty with the Appleby family ever since.

Yes! We flogged all the fish from the van and Dad got an extra three farthings for all the filleted bones for a lady's cat (she had lots of cats) but it was them oysters what Dad never flogged, not one. He was so sad.

We finished our fish round at about 12.47pm and Dad went to the pub. I played in adjacent bombed out cellars and caught tadpoles. At tea time I can remember the old man scoffing gleefully his box of oysters. He offered us boys some – safe bet for him, the sight of them made us feel sick – so we had none. I recall, though, just the zest of sea shore, lemon, black pepper, butter and brown bread.

I got my first blood blister next morning whilst hammering the shells up for our hens.

I fast forward: It is 41 years, 4 months, 6 days, 7 hours, 22 minutes later (or thereabouts).

Sigrid at last re-introduced me to oysters. She'd bought two dozen at Orkney Seafayre in Finstown. I'd never opened one. Never glubbed one down as Dad had. Sigrid was nudging me into a new era. If Sigrid was Eve and oyster and apple, "where would we be now?" I ask myself.

She handed me a dish cloth to wrap around my hand to protect it as I gripped the shelly comestible. Then a small, sharp, sturdy, pointed knife like Lotte Lenya's in 'From Russia with Love' to wrench them open with. My beloved showed me the oyster's weak spot, a tiny gap between top and bottom shell. Just there the knife point is pushed sharply in and skewed from left to right, thus severing living mollusc from its homely carapace. The knife is then twisted mercilessly to force upper shell from lower, revealing the delicious incumbent reclining in its now semi-detached residence.

With regular practice this operation can be completed rapidly and painlessly, particularly if you don't stab your hand. One can quickly spot le huitre's Achilles Eel and slip 'Lotte Lenya's' tool in with deftness, thus completing the 'ouverture' in painless sharp mini seconds.

As we artistically arrange our oysters on an assiette we test these 'fruits de mer' for virility. Sigrid demonstrated by squeezing a mere zest of lemon on the bi-valve's frilly edge. If said oyster reacts by performing a visual contraction, Sigrid explained that it was fit and well and could be approved for consumption. This act is effected by lifting the shell and posting its contents into the gap twixt nose and chin. Mastication is not always necessary at this point. Perhaps only a little pressure from the tongue, which increases the sensations amongst the taste buds. Then a little swallowing motion, a smack of lips, a click of tongue and repeat the entire process adding a little black pepper if required.

The finest oysters in Europe are supposed to come from our Gallic neighbours. It is a well-kept French secret that they actually don't. When there was an oil tanker disaster off the coast of North West Spain the oyster beds of the French were not just 'top hole'.

We went to market in Gourdon in the Lot and found a cluster of locals expressing delight over the Fish Stall's excellently beautiful, succulent oysters ever. And they were vanishing fast as we got a look in. There, we instantly recognised some old 'friends'; we are certain that these were Orkney oysters from Seafayre at Finstown. We took some back to our kitchen and opened them in time honoured fashion, whilst executing this very task we felt sure we could smell the Bay of Firth in those two holes just above the oyster posting box. And a tasty reminder of home.

Footnote: For sufferers of 'S.A.D.' syndrome obey above instructions and devour half a dozen oysters for they seem to have something which replaces what one loses with the lack of sunshine. Spoots can have the same effect too.

10 It's a parsley nuisance

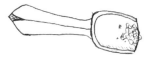

*'I came to slowly and gently. Sigrid asked me why I was
squawking in my sleep. "What, me, squawking?"
"Yes," she said very calmingly. "You clearly squawked."'*

On our long and enjoyable drive from France back to home in Orkney, Sigrid and I visited a series of friends and stayed a night or two here and there. Our first UK stop was at my pre-school friend's, Michael Hooper and his wife Chris. Our plan was to visit a Linklater and go round Penshurst Place with her.

Chris, sadly, developed stomach cramps and pains, so had to see her doctor. They caught up with us later, but Sigrid, Marie Louise and I were forced to wait in a Kentish Wealden pub where the bar food was exquisolently delicious. Eventually Chris and Mick arrived with the aid of continual guided directions from M L's mobile to 'The Rock' at Chiddingstone.

My haddock mornay will remain in my memory forever. I told the aproned Bartron that I would inform all my friends about his superb food. He replied dryly, "I shall expect the inundation then".

After lunch we went to Penshurst, a modest stately home with a great feeling of age, tradition and contentment. We wandered in the gardens with Chris ambling slowly and catching up occasionally. Her tummy pains were revolving around her stomach wall and it was not comfortable at all for her.

She managed very well though.

In these gardens I picked a wee herb or two and tried to divine a remedy. No joy at all. In any case we shouldn't interfere with the doctor's diligence, should we.

We departed from our friends the next morning for Yorkshire, thence to North Berwick for two nights and then all the way to distant St Monans for a stop (Notice the slowing pace while travelling northwards).

It was at Balgone House, North Berwick, when I first felt very slight 'ills of the Bell-Bells'. A troubling wee pain and an urge to visit one of Allan and Fidelity's many loos. Even for me I was excreetingly discreet. Nobody really noticed my sudden departures from table, why should they?

I would gently slip back into the friendly huddle of company as if nothing had happened.

On leaving N B in the east of Lothian we had business in Edinburgh.

My eyes constantly focussed on those matchstick man emblems which signify 'Male Toilet'. I headed and sometimes backed into these most welcome facilities. When incarcerated within I often mused: "Never mind, all things pass – and patience brings a better day" and then I jested to myself that on vacating this chamber this very tummy problem will abate.

In this situation abatement was a far off winsome dream. I was in a daymare. Timing and control were the keywords.

At Anne's cottage in St Monans, I oiled the squeaky hinges on the loo door, fixed the unpredictably noisy balcock in her echo chamber of a cistern, found where the creaky floorboards were and covered my sound traces. Sigrid was oblivious to all these goings on, just reminiscing with Anne.

When one has a 'problem' where all emissions are unpredictable and extremely liquid it is a brilliant idea to fast and fast quick.

However, on leaving Anne's pink cottage we headed for Dundee, then to Perth where we had a posh lunch invitation to a swish French restaurant with Margarita Carolina Georgette Chabotel-Krummer and Vivian (two people). It would have been rude to refuse. The Patron took our coats and hung them discreetly by the bog signs. Inner rumblings were quiet momentarily.

Our repast was of the finest order. Moules Marinière with a Pyrenean Basque influence and then John Dory fillets and black-eyed beans. With food like this one forgets one's little trifles - but they don't forget you.

I had to make a few swift exits to "blow my nose", "to clean my spectacles" I walked off an attack of "Le Cramp". One can be quite inventive when driven to it.

Anyway, later on, I found the loos on the Hamnavoe most engaging as we completed our last leagues home. On this craft I resolved to seek the aid of a professional medic, so on returning to the Pottery my index digit dialed the hallowed numeral thus: 7, 7, 1, 2, 0, 9. "Good afternoon, Dounby surgery" came the answer to my call. I appealed for an appointment. Sheila booked me in for ten minutes past four that afternoon. "And whit like Andrew?" she enquired. "I'm saying nuffing, in case it's construed rude" I replied.

My number was up. "Andrew Appleby to surgery one please". Behind that sépal portal awaited Doctor Hazlehurst.

Ever sympathetic he asked after my health. I explained in genteel detail my discomforts and he sighed. I was directed to the curtained couch where he dextrously examined my abdominal regions applying pressure to the painful parts wherever he could find them.

He said "Umm".

This I found very comforting indeed and I was ushered to the patients seat by his computer.

Doctor Bob explained to me that he needed a 'sample'. I rolled up my right sleeve ready for that blood sucking syringe. My Physician rolled up his eyebrows. "Not a blood sample Andrew"! So I poked out my tongue for him. "No, Andrew, not a saliva test". He handed me a diminutive transparent phial with a blue screw top lid. Protruding down from the lid and into that flask was a dinky little shovel thing, which was also in an attractive blue hue.

It so resembled one of those useful ice cream spoons one gets in individual tubs. This container was graded as a raingage is. "What's this for" I questioned. Gee. Pee. Bob hinted rather than succinctly explaining its purpose. His main directive, however, was: "Don't fill it right up. The lab only needs a small scrap".

I got the drift and worked it all out for myself. The sample was delivered by hand in a plain brown wrapper eighteen and a half minutes later.

I was prescribed no medication so spent the rest of the day and evening in my general discomfort and went to bed early.

Five twelve a.m. is the time when I have vivid, and sometimes foretelling, dreams.

I shall relate this pertinent one. It was September 1965, my Pottery tutor at college, Beryl Hardman, was telling me about her parrot who's name was Bird. Suddenly as dreams do, I was transported to Beryl's parlour. Bird was frantically and artistically stripping off Beryl's wallpaper in long, narrow vertical ribbons.

The paper was of a flowery pattern and the surface underneath was a fleshy pink shade. Bird was shrieking out "It's a parsley nuisance! It's a parsley nuisance!" and then she performed an impression of a high speed car crash, ambulance, police cars and fire engines. Bird lived on the north cicular and this was a regular occurrence.

I came to slowly and gently. Sigrid asked me why I was squawking in my sleep. "What, me, squawking?" "Yes" she said very calmingly, "you clearly squawked 'its Parsley for Nuisance, PARSLEY NUISANCE' or something akin." "Thank you, my bonny cherub, thank you," I yawned and drifted back to deep sleep.

Sigrid breakfasted at eleven minutes past eight - scrambled eggs, toast, coffee, I observed. En route from Stromness to the Pottery we stopped at Flett's Butcher's vegetable department where I bought their entire, but modest stock of fresh parsley.

I was still chewing some when we obeyed the speed limit in Stenness. Noticeably, by the time we reached Maes Howe and were turning into the Stoneyhill Road my tummy soreness had subsided.

On reaching the Pottery at eight forty-eight I was feeling quietly confident about the day ahead. I took a little more parsley and then a little less and felt weller by the minute.

The day was spent pleasantly recovering from my former gastric disorder. Parsley performed brilliantly as my bowels ceased performing summersaults.

Parsley, what a fine mess you've got me out of.

PS: Parsley is poisonous to Parrots. 'Parsley' was Bird's worst swear word ever.

11 Chivvie up with chives

'They assured me he had "all the prescribable and indescribable medicines and remedies possibly procurable, so: there was nothing more to do."'

I'm back to bairnhood again. Scoffing the 'onion grass', and loving it. I was then aged three and Mum would always know where I'd been. My breath 'apong' from my grazing. I had been on all fours pretending to be a buffalo on a munching mission, muzzling in the herb border, devouring CHIVES.

(Nothing has changed.)

When I was older, much, much older, perhaps even eleven (odd this! who recalls being eleven, even?) Actually it was in August, so I would have been 10. However it was when my cousin Simon visited our home. It must have been a formative moment for him. I showed him my specially delicious pass time: chive grazing!

I was a buffalo again. Boy cousin, a 'he calf'. Very soon I was in 'heap big trouble'.

Simon's granny (my aunt Dorothy, or 'Doffrey), caught us. I got humunguously scolderated by my father's sister from Brighton – well, Hove actually. I was made to feel like a guilty lamb.

Doffrey, and Jen, my first cousin (who was not going to be removed) seconded her mother into a loftier position, where she continued first hand reprimands. Personally, and I can only assume for my benefit, thus scolded, I remained shriven. Thyme's a great healer.

And now chives retain sublime memories for me, and I cannot live without them, as others cannot exist with a complete dearth of capers.

Chives chopped and added to scrambled egg at the final moment of cooking create bliss at breakfast. Garnishing a steak or simply tossed with a green salad: delightful. No wonder clumps of chives are dotted about the Pottery garden.

One early June morning, a Shetland couple and their son visited our Pottery. Poor, poor lad. He was a look-alike for a mixie rabbit, eyes all puffed up and watering, nose sore, itchy and swollen. He was in pain. His sympathetic parents excused their afflicted son's appearance by telling me that he had 'hay fever'.

I asked if I could get him anything. A positively negative reply eminced forward. They assured me he had "all the prescribable and indescribable medicines and remedies possibly procurable, so: there was nothing more to do".

I pondered, as one does: "Where there's an allergy, there's an antidote." I mused again. "Nature provided this balance, so something will verily be divined."

My own chives were flowering and I could visualise them in my mind's eye. I said to my visitors: "Wait just there". I then gambolled to my potagé and plucked a handful of those beautiful amethyst blooms.

On my return I asked his parents if he'd chew five chive flowers.

"He will try anything, he's that desperate," they informed me.

Poor lad, he looked so weary. "The dose," I said to him, "is five chive flowers". He snatched the whole lot, though trembling at the prospect. This quintessential floral suite entered my 'guinea pig's' gob.

As he chewed, I counselled him thus: "Breathe in through your mouth gently. Inhale that ether of Allium down to the depths of your lungs."

He complied. "Now, hold on and keep your breath for several moments, then, gently release through your nose."

I continued: "Keep chewing and continue this rhythm." He did.

Maa & Daa then chatted about pottery and were choosing a few things. I thought that they may have been wondering if I had been doing something barbarous to their son and were in the very strange company of a complete wierdo.

Surprisingly, No! They carried on as if all was normal.

A few minutes later, when I was wrapping up their pottery, the lad asked, "Oh! Mum and Dad, can I get one or two of those beasties – a bookmark?" Dam and Sire turned to their progeny, agape. He hadn't spoken voluntarily for three days.

His voice had rung like crystal. They observed, wide-eyed, his countenance, which was now soothed. His eyes were returning to normal as his tear ducts ceased their soreness.

Our quartet were ecstatic with this rapid recovery. This loon implored for further medication.

I warned against overdosing, durst the floral tributes may be exhausted. However, I was able to procure a further bagful of blooms to be kept fresh in their self-catering fridge, also a chive root or two.

As it happened they had chives growing by their back door, and son could pro-cure himself any time.

I heard later that he was needless of pills – sachets, nostril sniffers and other very expensive potions which only made him drowsy and fatigued, especially at exam time, and sluggish when he should be spritely.

This was when I coined this still unknown phrase: "Rather a fist full of flowers than a fist full of dullars".

Hay fever season is now upon us. Our chives are burgeoning, like the mint, at the pottery. Preparing themselves for their healing duties like Florence Nightingale.

Their compact flower buds are formulating their remedies thus: Natural pollen, which you ingest (many a true word is spoken in jest) and inhale, a portion of nectar and manifold medicinal elements, perhaps even natural antihistamine, encapsulated in these pharmaceutical buds.

Should you choose to chew the chive in this way, then all these goodies will rapidly enter your bloodstream through your digestive organs and stomach linings (tripe).

Your wind pipes will offer the ether to pulmonaries and your system will be alerted with internal early warning culminating in the strong defence of an attack.

Your body will have all guns blazing with bags of ammo to repel pernicious pollen invaders.

It is as simple as that.

If you have recalcitrants who will not take their medicine: simply chop up chive flowers in a salad and serve. Garnish boiled new tatties similarly. Shove them in a 'shanwidge'. Whichever way you get them taken, nurse C Flower will get curing.

PG certificated. This can be read during meal times.

12 A burgeon of mint

'Mint was on the mind. I remembered Madge, my mother, chopping mint leaves and teaching her infant the task.'

Sigrid only revealed that morning that she'd secretly purchased some Orkney lamb, cut into conveniently dicey chunks.

She announced this because she had observed me rummaging to the bottom of our deep freezer, searching ardently for those grotty bits I'm so fond of. Sometimes a wee poke of freezer-burned gizzards, or even a boney corner of a road-killed rabbit, projecting from its punctured polybag.

"No", I said to myself, "take pity, have consideration – be thoughtful," for my sweetheart had provided for us 'store-bought' messages to be enjoyed without the faintest fear of enduring one of my kerbside concoctions.

We'd only just arrived back from the very successful and enjoyable Country Living fair in Glasgow. This was our first morning home. On our drive north we went tadpoling in my brother's pools in Perthshire. This sport was an immense pleasure and our jarred infant amphibians journeyed obliviously to our petite pond ahindt the Pottery.

On releasing these tiny black, wriggling crotchets, to quiver and quaver, beating time in unison with their twirling tails, we turned from this wet little spectacle. Then Sigrid and I spotted our burgeoning bucket of mint.

That zinc-plated vessel was home to this, our first picking of a favourite herb. Every single thirtyseven fronds that I wrested from their parent plant were encaserated temporarily in a light blue polythene bag, along with a grand plucking of newly got wild garlic leaves and flower buds.

By mid morning, evening tea had been planned, and the

business of the day could be concentrated on.

Throwing lists, packing orders, letters, phone calls and finishing off a puckle of errands before even touching a dod of clay - at last I could work on a pot or two.

This is when the mind can wander and ponder. Clay revolves and the Potters' instincts tame and trim the turning tump.

Mint was on the mind. I remembered Madge, my mother, chopping mint leaves and teaching her infant the task. A simmer in a pan with a little Sarsons and a sprinkling of Tate & Lyle. Then allowed to cool in our wee cut glass jug and that was Sunday's roast shoulder's sauce.

I've learned a little more now. When the mint is growing apace and faster than you can control it, chop it down, smash it into tiny bits, shred it until it is so crushed it can't move. Shove it into a saucepan with a little cider vinegar, just enough to moisten the mint, then a splash of wine.

Put on a low light and clap a lid on, preferably a glass one so you can see the mint sweating.

It is not desirable to boil your essence, only a mere simmer. Turn the mint, stir a little so it simmers lightly and evenly. Add just a little Orkney honey, stir once more and allow to moulditude. Turn off the heat to cool.

When your superbly and gently simmered menthe is cold, pour into a jar, pot or jug and put in the fridge. This will be your base for mint sauces for the rest of the summer, or until it's gone.

It will keep in the fridge whilst it matures week by week, always improving.

You can use a spoon of this mixed into cous cous. A hint of mint in tea and an iota on buttered new tatties. Remember, it doth get tastier through time, so make lots.

Meanwhile, back to Sigrid's lamby choppy bits. We scissored up our tender minty fronds, stalks and all, cleaved our wild garlic sprouts, then stirred them into the simmering chunks of ruminant's flesh. The mint as an ingredient rather than a herb, just as the red and yellow peppers were delicious and refreshing.

We sometimes roast lamb shanks with bunches of mint swathed amongst them, all goes crispy, crunchy and munchy.

A few shallots which caramelise and create a sticky minty sauce, along with a burned roast parsnip and carrots. All cooked in one dish – it saves washing up and tastes - well, you try it.

Another hint for mint is "The Hangover Elixir" – simply go out into the dewy garden with no shoes or socks on. Pull up some mint, thrash it, shove it into a pint glass, add ice cubes and slices of cucumber and fill with cold water.

Contemplate it for one minute and fourteen seconds then drink. Repeat performance twice more. Then you can feel extremely virtuous and tell friends and family how truly well you feel, really I assure you it rarely fails.

Mint squished up and rubbed on your face will repel gnats and midges.

Also put some in a tiny vase in the fridge. It hides those 'petite pongs' in the cooler and the freshness is breath giving.

13 The charms of chickweed

'She was cornered, but at any moment she could strike like a cobra. I stared into her eyes and gave her the sternest ever look I have yet mustered.'

I shall start this with a complete irrelevence; if you fail to find a good beginnickle to an article then try sheer irrelevence. It can be a great device. Well! Here it comes. I am the proud new owner of a computorie lap toppy thing with a georgeous, dinky, colour inky printer.

Saint Peter of Easterquoy, my tutor was showing me the delights of 'Spell cheque' – it queried 'Appleby' and said 'try apoplexy'. I told Montague, my computor, that I'd been trying that all my life. 'Appleby' was then logged in. Montague F F Chizelhunt's Dictionary unsullied for eternity.

The point of my tale I must now come to. No longer can I put it off.

I have always enjoyed the colour, texture and taste of chickweed. It seems so fresh as it grows in the veg patch, particularly in August. I wonder why it's such a late developer. Maybe the gardeners have got tired by then and it gets a look in. Its light green foliage looks so bonnie against brown moist tilth after the tatties have been lifted, or amongst the onion patch.

I always felt a sadness when pulling it up and composting it. This 'weed' keeps the soil beneath it damp and cool, even under Orkney's Saharan sunshine.

It prevents the great American dust bowl effect too when the September gales hit us. These are only two good reasons to retain it if it isn't strangling its other co-habitants of the plot.

Now ... here comes the excellent reason for nurturing it ... exczema ... It is a very good natural solution to the problems caused by this irritable and debilitating condition. If you do suffer from this just pray that you can lay your hands on this plant. It is as soothing as its pleasant colour suggests.

Here's how it can work for you. Run yourself a hot bath, put a bunch of chickweed in a pot of water and boil said contents. You will end up with an appetising green liquid – pour some in a cup. Tip the rest – weeds and all into the bathwater and stir the soup until evenly dispersed. Enter your delightful pondlike bath with your warm chickydrinkie. Immerse yourself and sip your chickweed tea.

Count slowly to 447 whilst you relax in your stew.

Do not use soap. Relaxation is important in the relief of exczema.

If you suffer really badly and simply can't stay in the bath for long, then just have a quick dip. If this is too much then gently sponge yourself with chickweed water, and drink some too.

You will find this gives relief and you will, ... Bad Sufferer, ... be able to spend longer in the bath and attain this magic 447 count. One very important tip. Don't dry yourself, except for between the tootsies for it is better to leave essence of chicky stuff on your skin to help its healing hands.

Emma, my summer helper (this will be her 14th summer) was suffering from a typical and nasty 'irritable skin syndrome'. This meant that her slaving duties at the Pottery were considerably impaired, and that would never doooo.

I approached her whilst she toiled, painfully, at only 24.5 percent efficiency. "Emma," I enquired gently and sympathetically, "how are you feeling, poor soul?"

"Grouchy and *** horrible," came her response. As I noticed my profits beginning to slump, my brow furrowed a little. (This, however, made me look very caring.)

"I think I have a cure for your ills, dear, faithful worker," I informed her.

"Not those four lettered chives?" she queried.

"No, Emma, not chives ... chickweed."

"No!" she exploded. "Chickweed – that's compost stuff!!"

"Emma," I consoled, "why don't you go up into the mezzanine and have a wee rest. Put your feet up and dream a while."

"OK" came her weary reply, for pain is tiring.

She climbed the conveniently placed flight of narrow stairs to the creaky gallery above the workshop, she slumped herself in the sofa and put her feet up on the Chrystal Clear Lemonade crate conveniently poised close by. Emma never suspected a thing.

"Cumfy?" I called.

"Aye" came the answer. I detected a slight yawning quality in the start, middle and end of the word "A...Y...E."

This 'I', (me) slipped out to Harry Garriock's garden, conveniently close to the Pottery. I had formerly espied chickweed protecting his onions from the sun's glare. I gathered a Cummings and Spences placky pokefull and returned potwards.

I discerned a zizzzing sound. Emma had clocked off in the sofa. Dreams of boyfriend Naill, their pet hamsters and the little goldfish they so lovingly share.

All readers, please, say "AAAAAA-AAARHHRR."

As quietly as I could I climbed the stairs. Emma's rings in her nose were jiggling wrythmically in her breath as she inhaled nasally and then exhaled. Shortly, though, her mouth dropped open, dispelling the previous charming scene completely. I shan't describe the latter, as I wish you, reader, to retain the former image unshattered and not experience the one I suffered.

I put a bundle of chickweed in my electric kettle in our bijou kitchenette. I filled the sink with warm water. I depressed the kettle switch. The water within simmered and boiled. Russell Hobbs switched himself off, and I let the brew stew.

Emma stirred, wakened and whiped the dribble from her lower lip and chin.

"What's thou dooing" she enquired as sleep tried to take her back to her aquatic and furry musings.

"I'm making you that cure Emma." Quick as a flash she was up and making for the stair.

"No! Not on your herballists ******** Nelly." It was the way she screeched "Her–ball–ists" that was so frightening.

I leapt and headed her off, forcing a retreat from stairhead to Russell. She grabbed the vacuum pipe and waved it at me. "Phew!" Lucky for me it fell apart leaving only the plastic screw attachment to lunge with. The pipe rolled, inconveniently, out of reach. She was cornered, but at any moment she could strike like a cobra. I stared into her eyes and gave her the sternest ever look I have yet mustered. Emma gave in and said, "O.K. Doc., the game's up. I'll come quiet."

Yes, I thought, but be wary – be on you guard, Andrew.

"Show me your hands Emma." She did, first one, then the other. "See ... no weapons," she told me.

"Indeed," I replied, "but I observe a soreness of your hands which concerns me, maybe exczema, or one of its friends or rellies."

I poured some of the CW tea into her favourite mug, an Andrew Wilson Silver Jubilee piece. "What's that for?" Em asked tremblingly.

"That's for later," came my informative reply. I poured the rest of Hobbs' weeds and all into the sink.

"Now, Emma," I commanded, "steep thee mits in that special brew."

Her sore palms and digits dibbled gingerly at the concoctions edge. "In. Emma." She regarded me, cowed. She slowly immersed her hands and then actually brightened up a little, conversing with words of one, two and three letters up to seventeen, but omitting all fours and never once uttering "Herballists".

"Now Emma, count slowly backwards, out loud, from one hundred and eighty three, to one."

"All the way?"

"Yes Emma, all the way, and leave your hands in sinky whilst you do it."

I made myself a drink of Marmite in my favourite Andrew Wilson Jubilee mug, with a delightful sketch of him on a 'Penny Fart Hing'.

"Three – two – one – hands up! Don't dry them," I warned. She eyed my mug and then its brim-filled twin. "Now Emma, drink" "Won't"..." You must Emma ... It's part of the cure." "Cure," she veheemed. She did, however, take the mug, sipped, spat and said: "Boggy".

"Emma, please, just a little. Do try. It works." She tried once more (bless her), and faked a swallowing sound, but a little went down. Then – asplike, she struck, pushed me aside and flung the rest down the nearest convenient sink.

Emma phoned me at home later that evening. Her digits were back to normal and the irritation was gone.

PS. There is an Orcadian lady who bides in Edinburgh. She's confirmed the sheer relief of the charms of chickweed.

14 Weed, Weed, little Weed

'At the checkout, she checked me out, I confessed to my "rendez vous" or "rondequa" I think she was a little surprised, but not totally.'

By the Flowerpot Man.

I used to be one of those really heavy smokers, always puffing with a fag in each hand, one in my mouth and perhaps another smouldering in some stained, grotty ash tray somewhere. I actually hated smoking and at times I really wanted to quit. I tried all sorts of ways, bribing myself with £5.00 a day if I didn't smoke. I once got to £35.00. A WHOLE WEEK! So what did I do? Yes, stupid me, I celebrated with just one FFffag... a favourite fag – a Benson and Hedges. Of course I had fully intended to give the rest of the packet away, but with the beer and 'Bonne homie' at the Pomona, one fag turns into two, with the sincere intention of then packing up again the next day. On the draw of the first cigarette, (factory-rolled to perfection, with care and special attention to quality), that wonderful rush of nicotine, taken directly into the blood stream, enters the brain. Just what the addicted cerebrum craved. (Craven Aye) The first puff-load of drug circulated. The addiction kicked back in.

Here the addict lies to his or herself. You think that you can handle it. Another puff, but the thrill is not quite the same. Never mind, perhaps the next time, but there you are, "Stupid old Fagginhand" You muse,,,,, the relaxation is good for you------- the ambiance`````` the nostalgia:::::: The comfort ^^^^^^ The curl of the smoke, blue, grey and wispy.... The glow of the tobacco when you first light it = = = = the sadness when you stub it out. The smouldering friend crushed by its filter, perhaps even being drowned by a few drips of spilt beer in the ashtray.

All these things go to reinforce the smokers' beliefs that fags are friends and it is quite ok to smoke. This is the addiction lying and tricking the smoker, his or her tobacco 'Anchor'; a 'Bachelor' married to weed.

Breaking the 'HABIT' therefore, is very difficult... The 'HABIT' – NO! It is not a habit; it is plainly and simply a terrible addiction.

Tobacco plants look gorgeous in the fields, like giant Cos lettuces they are. Sigrid and I winter in a tobacco growing area, so we see them still being cultivated, though on an ever-decreasing scale. We arrive just before the harvest. The fields are cleared and the crop removed to attics or special drying barns. Our own loft, or grenier, is equipped with wires and vents for just this purpose. The farms around us provided tobacco for great curly cigars, tobacco for hand rolling and for fine cigarettes. I can now look on it all from a safe distance.

A couple of our neighbours rise early for work. I hear them coughing and hawking in the morning mist. Their father has had a lung removed because of smoking. The sons are tricked by their addiction that they are totally immune to their Pop's affliction. They are very pleasant sons who work hard and very well at their business. They come in for apéritifs sometimes and seem sad when I refuse their offers of a smoke, as others do. Their sadness is in not recruiting another comrade in harms, to make them feel more comfortable and bolstered in their chained trap. They cannot get me to share their breathing in of extinction just to make them feel better.

Sigrid and I got engaged about twelve years ago. I wanted our forthcoming marriage to last a very long time. This meant health, moderate fitness, and long life. Not a coughing, dieing addict, clutching on to last breaths, with tubes sticking out of orifices and arteries... Not a pretty sight. Also before this terminal stage, the possibilities of emphesczemia, gangrene, painful varicose veins, dead taste buds and a pallid, wrinkly complexion. None of these things I wanted to give her as a wedding expectation... So, what did I do??? You've got it... I resolved to stop.

I kept my resolution a secret, because, I felt this I had to do on my own. With so many failures before, I didn't want to share disaster and cast blame. I had to prepare myself... First I gave up hand rolling my fags and treated myself to those Bensons again. Ceasing to hand roll removed the dexterous pleasure that I would derive from the preparation of my next nail in the coffin. (All the nails will go in one day, but not by my hand). I would enjoy my last few packets of golden, flip top boxes,,,comforting to open... Tightly packed`````` crisp, clean smokes... like bullets in a box.

Unbeknownst to Sigrid, I had set the fuse on my petite 'bombshell'. We were travelling back from Edinburgh when I announced that I was "seeing someone" and she would have to wait for me in Inverness whilst I broke off an "auld alliance". I would rejoin her at 16.37 hrs. that afternoon. This gave me sufficient time to visit the __HYPNOTHERAPIST__ I had two more fags, or eighteen less Bensons to consume. My penultimate in the car... The ultimate at the bottom of the practitioner's pitch path. A last screw of toe on stub and I ventured up the tarmacad'am strip to his red brick doorstep...

Roll on part two... coming soon.

PPPPpppppPart Two

You remember the first episodic bit of 'Weed, Weed, little Weed,' by that potter chap, don't you? Well here comes the next bit. If you are a smoker, or just want to help one off the hook, then CUT THIS ARTICLE OUT. I have asked the Editron in Chieftainship to put one of those scizzorie gismos and a dotted line round this article, so he'd better had.

CONTINUATION—!!!!!

I put one foot on the red portal, which had the hue of lipstick on a fag-but. I touched the doorbell with my nicotined index digit. I exerted the required pressure to dong the dinger, and the door swung open, independent of any other hand. Surely, I had gone to the wrong address, so I was ready to turn on my heel when a voice said, "Mister Appleby, you are right on time."

"Ning!!!" I expressed to myself.

Christopher, the hypnotherapist showed me into his "surgery". A comfy, swingy, leathery armchair beckoned me from the far corner. I sat in it. Hypnodoc announced that it was his chair, but I was very welcome to use it. He leaned against the couch. I felt very at home in the seat of my choice.

We chatted a bit about ourselves. He told me how he got into Hypnotherapy, and I told him how I was trying to get out of it. Here came his first bit of cheer, he said "People who smoke, often say that the therapy won't work on them, they are too far gone." This is

41

just how I felt. He added "Andrew, you are here aren't you? Nobody forced you up my path. It was you that put one foot in front of the other, wasn't it?" I had to agree. This helped me a lot; it made me feel more in control. Although I was unsure whether this would work or no, but I knew that there was a chance if only I would allow it.

I was played some very soothing music through a set of headphones. This was to relax me. I tell you, I can go sound asleep in a barber's chair with Radio Two annoying me as my wig is being trimmed. This was deep watery music with gentle bubbly bits, where you imagine swaying pondweed and the odd angelfish slipping by, (It nearly had me in a coma.) Actually, I was completely conscious, was able to think and daydream, drifting from one musing to another. (A bit like work, actually)......Then Chrisnotherapits began telling me an ever so gentle tale. It was nothing to do with smoking at all. Anyway it was such an innocent and mildly interesting life story of a Paperboy who delivered the news to the houses around. There was a particularly attractive house that he really liked, but as a young lad, he knew it was a completely far off dream for him to aspire to. He grew to be an adult and became the manager of the paper shop... I won't spoil the story for you, but every word was chosen in the script for gently analysing, and as the weeks went on after my session, I discovered the symbolism of each phrase and turn of a word.

I paid the fee, forty quid. Left the 'Maison Therapeutique' and went to meet my beloved in deepest Inverness. We did shopping! I only wanted to buy fruit. Sigrid did ask where I had been. At the checkout, she checked me out! I confessed to my 'rendez-vous' or 'rondequa'. I think she was a little surprised, but not totally. Proof positive... At the fag counter, I made no purchases. She knew I was low on B&H... I glanced at the attractive looking packets, but could see right through them. The lady at the counter was only doing her job. I do hope she was sorry for her clientele. There was a small queue of customers contemplating their purchases, rehearsing their requests in their minds for the drug, putting their corpsssssessssssssss aside from their proper consciousness. — I went.

From then on I have always felt a great sorrow for the smoker.=+ Their lives in jeopardy.+= Their discomfort when small afflictions unnecessarily take to them.=+ The cough which they can't throw off.=+ The dry skin.+= The tongue tasting like the bottom of a parrot's cage.=+ The roof of a mouth feeling like Long John Silver's arm pit.+=

The panting at exertion. That inner feeling of unremitting suspicion that ones Wills Whiff would bind you to a lone Capstone!!!+=

We arrived home at the centre of the world, Harray, and got on with life. I had no problem with every day things. Smoking was a thing of the past. I felt I was giving Sigrid a better and healthier husband. I did not want to be a bigot over smoking. I was very happy to tolerate smokers and enjoy the scents of tobacco, that nostalgic aroma.

Days passed in joy and work, then, within my arms, I felt a tingling, which developed into a trembling..... Following this a tickle in the larynx......Complemented by a certain dizziness at times,,,,,,....;;Over the following days, unwelcome sudden headaches,,,,, crazy sensations in my Adam's Apple...>>>>>>Heart flutters not associated with romance, and all my tummy motions became "unpredictable". I rang the number ending in 209. I pleaded for the appointment, and was to attend at twelve minutes past 09.33 that morning. My absolute favourite doctor observed and listened to each and every complaint of symptom and gripe. He assessed, correctly, that I was cracking up. Maybe he had realised that I did not smell of tobacco anymore. I don't know, but there was a confession in the air... I told my GEEEE PEEEE that I had CEASED SMOKING. His beard wagged in front of his understanding chin, directed by that clever head of his. "I See. So when did you stop smoking?" himselph enquired. I confirmed: "Ten days and a bit ago." Never has the expression "Cold Turkey" been so relevant, when kind Dr. Hazlehurts explained that I required, and was desperate for HELP. His remedy, I took and respected... Patches... Nicotine Patches. They cost more cash than making ash, but it was certainly better.

I followed the directions on the pink packaging.... Slap one on yer arm for 24 hours. Remove and put another on. The rush of nicotine to the brain was so good... All my 'Cold Turkey' vanished. I felt like a warm turkey!!=-.All preened and ready for the day.-= So what I did was to forget to put the next one on 24 hrs. après, and left it until I was Craven. Perhaps 29 to 31 hrs 47 minutes later. The rush was good again. I knew that the addiction wasn't over, but with the aid of the patches, this was working for me.

Later I could scale down to smaller doses for a week or so, then even weaker ones. Finally, I totally forgot to put one on. The addiction was weaned away... The hypnotherapy re-enforced my own will to stop smoking. It all worked. The nostalgia of smoking has gone.

This all happened over eleven years ago. This has turned into a serious article now, but it is, after all not a flip-top flippant subject.

Yours Aye Andrew.

Post Mortem Script.
Our neighbour died of his lung cancer. His two sons quit that weed AND ARE WELL NOW. We have lost a very dear potter friend, Jean- Pierre Tejada Fernandes as direct result of tobacco smoking.

SIX-FOOT NOTE

SMOKING WILL GIVE YOU UP IF YOU DON'T GIVE IT UP FIRST.

15 Heavy light pollution

'Their harsh painful luminosity hits the visual senses.
Their reflection across the sea destroys a sense of well being ...'

Sigrid and I were invited oer the sea to Sanday. It was our "old Friend's" birthday doo. We duly sent a requestial dedicational tribute especially for Bill, via Fionn Mc.Arthur, of BBC Radio Orkney. We just got it in in time. Mister, newly wed, McArthur couldn't guarantee the lovely song we had specially chosen for this Grand occasion... 'OVER THE HILLS AND FAR AWAY'... but he got something suitably excellent from the Wyre Band... We missed the Transmission because we had to listen to the recorded voice of Himotherselph, Dave Grieve, also from R.O., giving all the arrival and warning announcements to say we were rapidly closing in on the Loth Pier.

I think that you, reader, are thinking: "Irrelevant! What's he going on about?" Well, I'm only trying to set the scene, the picture, and the geography of the whole situation... So, please be very patient with me, and decipher on.

It was still early evening when William met us on secure, dry concrete. 'Yard-arm' hadn't been reached, quite yet. On arrival at Headbanx, Sun was dipping towards its evening goal. 'Toast' had arrived. Bill's health was assured as we sipped.

Birthday "tea" was to be at Pool in Bill's recently acquired retreat. What a work they had done. This bare but-and-ben, treated to care and love === all looked so beautiful. The table laid for a throng.

Guests arrived, including the parental elements of young Fionn, and a meal, sumptuous in all departments and courses was taken pleasure in. The extricables of time flowed. So the indulgents needed leg exercises. The solar course had declined below our horizons... DarK

WaS ThE NighT.

What quiet and peace descended around us; from the waxen candle glow, to the pitch of sunless, moonless, star-studded BLACKNESS; a carpet of dark that soothed the soul. Stars, Nebulae, Constellations, Planets, Asteroids, Meteoroids, distant nameless moons granted the glimmer which we accepted. This Dark of nature allowed eyes to adjust, pupils to pupate, and irises to open. Glad were we as dark revealed shape, tone, reflection, hue, and perspective. Sigrid commented that even I looked "Nay Too Bad" in this dimness of ours.

"Natural Nightlight" is what we deny ourselves. Who in Kirkwall has seen the Light of Night recently??????????........Think about it. This is one of my hobbyhorses, and I'm still riding "bare back" on it..... STREET LIGHTING...... I think it is purely shocking that those terrible orange, fiery, torches strike the night sky and POLLUTE it, HEAVILY. Who ever sees the Merry Dancers in Warrenfield, Who observes the Milky way from Kiln Corner. Who detects the Moon's Brough in School Place? Please let me know.....

Our orange street lamps do not emit a natural light. The colour radiating from them is not conducive to peace and tranquillity. Subliminally they create a state of unease in people. It is quite probable that they enhance an inner sense of anger in folk. All this sounds weird. But, do acts of vandalism occur in dim, dark places, or daylight???? Not so much, I guess.

White, or pale yellow lighting is peaceful. Gentle light shone downwards, illuminating what we need to be lit. If light is contained and not allowed to flood the sky with its infectious rays, then we have a chance to see the stars. They will look down on us, as they always have, even through a clouded night sky they will still have some effect.

When I see those Orange beacons, ever blaring from Rousay Pier, they affront me. Their harsh painful luminosity hits the visual senses. Their reflection across the sea destroys a sense of well being, so much  so that I have been heard to scream out "BOREALIS" a lot.

The lights of San Fran Finstown! Costa Del Dounby! Puerto St.Romness! Orphir-on-Sea! St. Margaret's Del Fuego! Surely, by a little sense and adjustment, we could have calm, clear dark in our night vistas.

What about Kettletoft le Spa? Hatston de Charme?

Flotta-cum-Harmony? All these aspirations are plausible... Ration the rays, bend the beams, guide that glimmer to just where it is needed. Planners should plan, planners should look, planners should listen. PPPPPPPPPPPPPlannnnnnnnnnnnnners will then be congratulated when light is seen to be done.

HERE ENDETH THE TIRADE

Yours Aye Andrew +(I'll add in 'Of the Lamp')+

Photograph by John Ross Scott

16 Mustard

'Don't get flustered, you'll ruin the mustard'

When I was wee, Sunday lunchtime was one of those blessed, or perilous occasions. Dad had either been out shooting with uncles and friends, or been for a drink or three at the BooZeR, usually both. Madge (Mum) had been sweating in the kitchen cooking the remains of whatever was shot the Sunday before or, even better still, something Dad had bartered for from the butchers. We never bothered with the "Meat Coupons." We swapped them or traded them.

Well! That was the life; fish round, picking mushrooms on the common, plucking pigeons. I could write a thesis on 'GIZZARDS' – digression is an art to a certain extent, but we have a SUBJECT>>> 'MUSTARD' – so I will try to get relevant.

Salt beef or, 'boiled beef and carrots', with old tatties, flabby looking onions and a dish of sprouts, was not appealing to me. However, a starving three year old, as I was, soon altered his opinion when the first warm, comforting mouths full passed my lips. Bliss. Dad would carve for the rest of the family. The firm slices parted from the saline silver side, glistening, almost with the bloom of a mackerel's skin. Each person was catered for.

Mum at last sat down for hers, Dad had his cutlery poised 'Mustard!" he'd yelp. "where's the bleedin' Mustard?" Mum, guilt stricken, would make for the kitchen. We'd hear the clatter in the cupboard, the Colman's tin striking the enamel surface of the 'Easywork'. Madge would hurriedly tip the powder into the very inconvenient 'Düsseldorf' mustard pot. In the rush she'd pour too much milk in it.

(Dad absolutely insisted on milk) Extra yellow dust entered the mix from that sharp edged tin. Oh! No! It went all lumpy. We'd hear this kitchen sink drama through the thin brick partition wall; Dad with his Sunday Lunch cooling, and his temper heating – us boys trying not to notice. Our deaf grandmother, Daisy, issuing table manner tips, whilst her hearing aid screamed over her devoid breasts.

We could distinctly hear the worn metal spoon revolving at the speed of sound in that Germanic china paste vessel. The mix would just begin to blend as Madge did her 're-entry' to the heavy atmosphere of the dining 'salon'. Mustard was gingerly placed right to the Master's left. The spoon, hot from Mater's exhausted fingers, transported said condiment to pater's platter. Bang! Bang! Then, 'Little Bang!' went the implement, thus shedding its load on his dish's rim.

The "Mustard" row then ensued. What we learned, or didn't learn about mustard remains to be seen. Grandmother, 'Daisy' (nicknamed 'Beetroot') joined in. She could hear now!! Madge noticed that our plates were empty, and her sons needed replenishment. The 'Old Man' had to carve more whilst going on about allowing mustard to soak and settle, 'mebbee' 2 hours before serving! We'd ask Beetroot to pass the mustard. She'd shout "Speak in the box" and continue on about "manners", Dad's tirade would slowly subside as he settled into his cold meat, quietly uttering "BU*******!! >>> Ruined" (We all knew what "Ruined" meant.)

Here we learned that mustard should be allowed a while for maturation. I have found the truth of this. Strong English mustard can have a very harsh under-taste, which spoils peoples' enjoyment of it. I never use milk to mix mustard; it just doesn't keep well with 'cow juice' It soon goes dry and solid. I well remember the light yellow softness in the middle of the pot, and the tanned hard remains on the rim, not to mention the concretion adhering to Madge's poor whipping spoon.

DECADES LATER...

SORRY...

MANY DECADES LATER!
Whenever us brothers meet, we usually, or to onlookers, unusually, re-enact the 'MUSTARD' drama. Sigrid was one of those 'onlookers'

– I must say, she passed the family test. So, at our wedding buffet several months later, we had some interesting varieties of mustard. We used cider vinegar, Noilly Prat, Beer or Whisky with which to mix the powdered herb. These ingredients assist in the preservation of the condiment, and enhance the flavour.

To dilute the strength we add mayonnaise, thus creating a gentle cold dressing. We also add crushed garlic, chopped walnuts, capers and sometimes, sunflower seeds. We put in poppy seeds, too, which swell up; this can stiffen the mix if you mucked it up with too much Vermouth for instance. Dad was right about timing; you can correct mistakes artfully if you have time. Dry mustard seeds strewn in to a 'runny mix' can absorb that drop too far of Eau de Vie, therefore each single little seed, re-hydrated with beverage, can be a veritable taste bomb.

Powdered English mustard (And I'm not being paid for this) The Coleman's variety is so versatile. Vinaigrettes would be virtually impossible without it. Welsh Rarebit; gentle mustard sauce; poltices. So many things; so many uses. Shove some mustard powder in your wellie boots and you'll not get cold feet!!!

As kids, we often wanted worms for fishing. We always got yelled at for digging up the flowerbeds; so we had to think "laterally." We prised open that tin of dusty sunshine, tipped the contents into a brimming watering can, stirred until fully and evenly dissolved. We then selected the juiciest bit of our back lawn. Evenly, methodically and meticulously we sprinkled that turf. A pallid, jaundiced, misty spray settled serenely on the cropped surface. Gradually the brew soaked downwards through the wormholes. To ginger this drenching we did the 'Dance of the Worm Dervishes'. The effect was tumultuous!>>> WORMS...WORMS... MORE WORMS..! This very rectangle, that patch, the chosen sector, exuded worms. Huge ones, long ones, shorties, stubby, fat ones, yellow, red, grey... All wriggling from their sypholes. Gleefully we grabbed them as they tried to escape their mustard bath. Joyfully they were garnered as we anticipated each

roach, rud, perch or pike that these worms would tempt for us. Then, piercingly, shrilly, in the midst of this hiatus, we heard Madge's screams from our kitchen.

"WHERES THE MUSTARD?!"

17 / New Year's note

'The absolutely crisp, clear, skies with the low sun reflecting over lochs, sea and ice ponds was a miraculous sight for me. The breeze rose as the fallen snow was blown into fans and filled a few dykes.'

Editron of all Editrons has demanded of me a "New Year's notelette" I hath pondered and pondered again and again over it. Is it to be about REZOLUTIONZzzZ? Should it contain hangover remedies? Homilies of the year past? Recipes for a successful 'Nouvelle Anné?' Perhaps all the "Bromides" that continually goes into other papers? I expect not!!! – if I am wrong, then this might be my very last 'Now and Then Note' to be published in 'ORKNEY TODAY'.

You may gather that I was born in Kent. My father spent a lot of his wartime in Orkney. He was with the Army Intelligence. There are many tales he told us of his treasured times here. James Rowan of Fursbreck Farm was one of his colleagues. They spent much time on Sanday at Tressness; they had an office at Red Roofs in Stromness, another at the Queens Hotel Kirkwall. There were so many stories he related to us bairns, all of these are secured in my memory. Tales of 'escapes' from the Italian prisoner of war camps. Embarrassing duck shoots. Spies, caught just by the slip of a tongue. Tales of Orkney hospitality and 'Teas' that would last for an afternoon, and then into the evening and late night with fiddle music and a squeeze box accompanying, and how the New Year went on for days and nights on end.

My father was really happy in Orkney; I feel that it was a great frustration to him that he couldn't spend his life here. He respected these Isles and those that bide here too... Orkney gave him the best time of his life, even though he had sailed round 'The Cape' in a clipper, ventured on the 'Shetland Bus' trafficked diamonds to

51

"Neutral" Sweden during his time in the Passport Office, socialised with German diplomats and other spies. He secured deals with "U" Boat builders up the Fjords of Norway and learned the gait of the Icelandic ponies. Orkney gave him what contentment he had. It is, therefore, not surprising, that two of his three sons live here now.

Of course we heard tales of those Hogmanays. The exchange of whisky 'by the neck', pocket warmed as you walked and visited neighbours on Work Head. That halfie which fitted the thigh in the trouser pouch, home brew' which should not really be mixed with it, (but sometimes was). Black bun, soda bread, bannocks, black bread, treacle, and oatcakes, drop scones, cold ham, clapshot.

I moved to Orkney in 1976. Dad's wartime friend, Jimmy Rowan of Fursbreck Farm, rented me his old chicken house to start my pottery in. My new neighbours, Peter and Joan Aim, gave me their friendship. They supported me and my venture with very kind help. My move to Orkney was a "Resolution" but not a new year's one. Andrew Wilson trusted me enough to let me have loads of stuff to wire my place up with and only pay for what I used. The Grimeston 'Toonsfolk' helped me through my culture shock and culture pleasure.

It was to be my first New Year in Orkney, still a virgin as far as that was concerned. What I do remember very well was the 'Chicken House' party I threw twixt Noel and 1st January1977. Everybody was speared to come, many did. The "Theme" was a darts match extravaganza, with Mack Smith on the organ. It was so cold! – so cold that we turned the kiln on full and opened its door. We cooked a vast pot of soup and enjoyed mince rolls with all the trimmings. (I had discovered that the twiglets had softened during the previous three months, so, alas they became crow food). Joan and Ronnie Robertson, from Tormiston Mill, saved the evening with a grand donation of mini vol-au-vents stuffed with kidneys and others filled with prawns. Everyone seemed to glow in the low light as the kiln took all the hydro.

Grimeston's New Year encroached. From Peter and Joan's house folk emerged after the midnight toll. Jim and Jackie Walter

from Nearhouse, Willie from Northouse, others:- some dead, but living with us still, gathered to make the rounds. We 'first footed' Bella O'Feolquoy, Mitchell Firth and Mrs. O' The Smiddy, a variety of the Gray Family, a Hamilton hoose and a Windywalls. Our 'happy wanderers' just seemed to go on and on, guiding me through the traditions, holding me up as I tried to get from one house to another, advising me to only pretend to take a tiny sip from the bottle neck, not SWIG. Yes!! A New Year Virgin, consummating and gestating with every sip of innocence, that veritable headache and hangover to be birthed on 1.1.77. That lesson hath lived with me ever since. I confess it has been learned, but not always remembered when it should have been best to. I find it a good idea to down a couple of pints of water before retiring. This irrigates the brain cells and washes poisons out which cause the headaches associated with an imbibing night.

By the third day of 1977 my heeid had cleared. A light dusting of snow had descended over Orkney. The absolutely crisp, clear skies with the low sun reflecting over lochs, sea and ice ponds was a miraculous sight for me. The breeze rose as the fallen snow was blown into fans and filled a few dykes. That evening, in the starlight, I decided to venture and do a visit or four on my own. In the first hoose, I was welcomed in for a dram. We clinked bottlenecks and sipped. Another "Newcomer" to Grimeston was there, visiting too. She explained that she needed guidance in this custom, as it differed from her homeland of Ireland in a few minute, yet significant details. I explained that I wasn't an expert at first footing yet, but we could always try. Muriel asked what might happen if we got it wrong. I replied, "He or she that makes no mistakes, makes nothing!"

We donned wellies and waded through fans, occasionally slipping in the soft walls of driven flakes.

I remember how we extricated ourselves from beneath the apex of one of those snowy crescents. It required a gentle recumbent rolling motion. The effect of this was to cover us with a light powdery dusting, which remained upon us as we entered Nearhouse Farm. Bella and Caleb remarked on our appearance as our snowiness was melting away, saying "Cold hands, warm hearts."

A little warming whisky, a few of Caleb's tall stories and it was time to depart. Bella remarked that we were all defrosted and dried out now. Mu replied, "Ah! But we have to go back that way, don't we."

That night there was a very deep frost. This preserved for eight days the tracks and evidence of our extrications... That was a very happy New Year indeed.

18 Road kill

*'There were telltale blood spots and shiny skid marks
on the pass. Searching our rear view mirror, I detected
no followers, so, it was very safe to halt.'*

Dear you who read me,

Sigrid and I left for our Southern wee hoose in Lot, France. Normally we drive (actually we do nothing "normally"). Ah! Ha! This time we had donated our very old, ancient, faithful Volvo to good friends who have promised to nurture her into a genteel and peaceful retirement on Sanday. (Less of that later)

Kneedless to say we travelled by alternative routes. IV.Jan.MMV at IX hrs a.m. on the Norflink ferry-boat Hrssy? Hjlpa? Not Sunnyph... Well, anyway, Knorphlynk passengered us Scrabsterwards from Hamnavoe. A gultch of yellow faces were braving the whipping tides and currents. Doggies, in far off canine quarters, resigning themselves to a sickening cruise, tails inextricably squeezed between hindquarters

A deep trough nearly secured my dear wife's incapacity through severe back injury by being thrown across the restaurant deck!!!. As is Sigrid's want, during her involuntary glide oer dispersing cutlery, the ship's china and doilies, she maintained the equilibrium of her coffee cup along with herselph. As if tiptoeing through the ether, she reached deck fall as a feather may touch a downy chick. Others may have been bruised... Her... No... Not a drop of caffeine lost, neither a single crystal of undiluted sugar, which remained dry and unsullied on her saucer.

We took the bus from the port of no return to Inverness. Montague Ff. Chizelhunt III my faithful laptop accompanied us. It was whilst approaching Golspie that we began to really miss our former mode of travel. For, there, just by a convenient lay-by and grassy verge, we espied a recumbent pheasant. There would have been plenty of room for us to pull in and collect that bird with our Volvo. I was so close to the driver of the charabanc we were cruising in but implore as I might, his duty forced him not to stoppP, only to drive relentlessly onward. Just so, he continued our fast-forward. Pheasant, duck, hare, escapee mink!! All were passed speedily by, vanished, vanquished; all to be mashed up by other traffic, or scavenged by diligent crows.

We were delayed at Inverness bus station for an hour; a toilet stop at 20pee a drip was duly paid for and appreciated. Then the second league of our journey was to commence. We arrived in Perth to stay with Marghareta, née Schabotelle-Khruemer-Montravaille, now Mrs. V Lineker and her new spouse, Mr. V. This is the moment when it really hit us. Usually we are so well provided with 'Spoils Of Tar McAdam' that, guests though we are, we are usually expected to be plucking, gutting, stuffing and preparing mortified feathered friends within minutes of entering our hosts' lodgings. Alas! No dead Dickies.

Margharita, or 'Rita' had to pull all the stoppps out. Viv pulled the corks. It was fortunate that they had a spare fatted calf for us to proceed upon. Well fed and contented we slept like little Yule logs. Next day we bussed it for Edinburgh, staying with rellies. A five o'clock a.m. start. An early taxi to the airport: One hare (On the wrong carriage way) and a pheasant close to our nearside. Far too fast and far too late to stop and reverse. (I've dreamt about that bird repeatedly.)

When we arrived at our Lot abode, after having flown by 'Sleasy Jet' and 'Cheapie Flight', we checked the runways for any 'Birdie strikes' ... but, nooooo, none, not even one. We thought we saw a phlegmingo as we circled round Carcassonne, but it was only the spitting image of a weather worn, obsolete Santa.

There have been so many times when we have been grateful for the 'Offerings of the Gravel' Items, garnered from the gutter. One in particular, a pheasant, close to death. (I made a mad rush for 'Pet Rescue' alas ... not in time! At least we didn't have to listen to a didjerie dooo). Late pheasant, as she was, we enshrined her in Baco Foil, and cocooned with her were five shallots, a libation of port and a crushing of garlic. Thus nurtured, she partook of the warmth of our oven. Never was a wild pheasant taken so much care of. Some boiled tatties mixed with celeriac (just like Clapshot, but fartier) 27 green beans steamed for sixteen and a half minutes, while her gentle roasting made its finale. This synchronised with the terminating of those propane flames 'neath her supporting cast. A more relaxed lady jungle fowl could not be enjawed in this Queendom.

One time, whilst progressing north, we were traversing the frozen glens. There were telltale blood spots and shiny skid marks on the pass. Searching our rear view mirror, I detected no followers, so, it was very safe to halt. My father had told us of the pleasures of Mountain Hares. The way they tasted of heather, juniper, wild cress, bitter and sweet herbs. Hares don't travel far after being hit. They haemorrhage quickly, their blood being thin causes this. In the mountains the hare will cool rapidly, but you must get it before it becomes "Crow Bait" .There, stretched out in a drift, I saw "Tufty" A very beautiful, high class, top quality white, mountain hare. Tufty, after a few hours of snowy climate, had become a firm friend. I released him from his frozen hillside sepulchre, and placed him aside our spare tyre. For company a lonely grouse joined him. At Blairgowrie we searched, in vain, for a Vet. Perhaps there was a last chance for that grouse, or maybe it was yet another hopeless case... So... finally Grouse was promoted to being an 'Ingredient', not a mere casualty.

I have to tell you that Snowy Hare, marinated with cider and port, stewed extremely gently for three hours with very old, tough, carrots, onions and 'StufF'. Then let to go stone cold... Then re-heated gently in the same pot two days later, was a Kingly Dish. You may well only ever have this once. So watch out as you traverse the Glens.

A rather strange 'Road Kill' we came across was a partan, half way up the Cairston Road. Not far past it was a neap, complete with its handle. We didn't cook these together. The way I cook a partan is, I think the kindest way, (if there is one.) Place said crustacean in a pot with about two inches of stone cold water, (before displacement takes place.) Gently lower 'Schelly' into the pan. Place vessel on the lowest light possible (Between 'Miser Rate' and 'Off') It is a kind notion to put a bunch of seaweed over crabby, it will make him feel more at home. (In any case little eight legs will taste much better.) Just leave

the pot. The water will warm very gently; this will caress your dweller of the deeps into a supperific swoon. When steam is visibly emitting from the pot, turn the gas up to 'Extravaganza' Allow water to ramp for eleven and three-quarters of a minute. Then, simply strain and serve hot. You will find this a cracking meal, and almost certainly the best crab you have ever tasted. The same goes for lobsters and even the humble shrimp.

Other finds have been a road kill loaf of Nimble bread, a bag of onions (much more welcome) a few tatties and once, a rue of peats. Our finest ever 'Kill' I thought was going to be a pigeon; Sigrid had been looking forward to one for ages. I was on my way to Finstown Post Office to annoy the mail sorters whilst I collected my letters. Well! There, close to the middle of the road was a lifeless feathered friend. I had sped past it, but not touched it. I couldn't stop because of the car behind. I checked the rear view mirror, and was relieved to notice that the following vehicle had not bruised the dickie either. I got my mail. I shot back to the scene. There, in pristine condition, was not pigeon, but wait for it, a Moor Hen! (I am always sorry to see crushed water birds like this, it makes me sad.) But this one was only slightly head butted. We had never had a moorhen before, so I treated this specimen with honour. I poached it very soothingly. We shared it with a leek sauce and a garnish of oyster mushrooms (All very watery). I can tell you that moorhen tastes like the aroma of an open water lily touched with celandine. It was an honour to have that experience. It will probably not happen again

In truth, I never try to hit a beastie with the car; I always take safe avoidance tactics when I can. The same goes for Sigrid. However we do do our kerb drill and keep a whether eye on that bountiful gutter... Bon Appétit... Yours, Aye, Andrew.

Pee. Ess. There was one time when I picked up a deer South of Golspie. I won't tell you about it, but I'm sure that if you book a taxi from Willie Corsie, (771 324) he'll delight in telling you all!

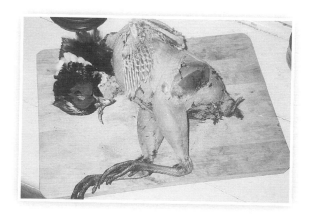

19 Whelks

*'At this Haven, at the bottom end of Brick Lane,
I could get, for a tanner, a gross amount of whelks,
peppered, vinegarred, then chewed'*

Just imagine it, Brighton Promenade (Well! Hove, actually) on a late September afternoon in 1955. My Grandmother, Daisy, (That regular reader of mine will be becoming familiar with Daisy) took me hand in glove for a walk along that reach. She took me to the "Groin", this is not what it sounds like, the GROIN was, and possibly still is, a long arm of concrete and granite with a spattering of re-used Portland stone from an earlier destroyed GROIN from the famous storm of eighteen hundred and wot's it.

My cooled mit was gripped by her suede and fur warmed digits. Fingers in fingers we walked against the wind out on to that Groin to watch the STORM. Daisy loved a good blow. Talk about Winter Gardens, this was Autumn Surfing. Thankfully we reached a barrier with a notice saying 'SEVERE DANGER – GO NO FURTHER'. At that time I was beginning to be able to read, we turned heel on heel and retreated as the surf followed us. Foam washed behind us and back through the culverts 'neath the protective abutments that might have just saved us had Daisy taken those few steps further.

At the head of the Groin, conveniently close to a bus shelter, was the Last Whelk Stall of Summer. Daisy extracted a three penny bit  from a distant fold in her purse and purchased a pint of those de-shelled helixes of nautical gristle. The penny three farthings change was counted and enshrined in her mothballed, calf skin safe. Encaserated in greaseproof paper and a sheet of the 'Sussex Times', the whelks, with Daisy and me were assisted by a strong Westerly to the bus shelter. I had on one of those faded Navy blue raincoats, which had been passed down from cousins to elder brother, and finally to me. I remember faintly the frayed strap and fallen eyelets of its belt, trying and failing to enknot with the Bakelite buckle, which had perished slightly several rainy summers before.

Seated on the wooden slats of the 'Shelter', we fought with the wrappings on our nude gastropods. The sweet smell of cold malt vinegar will forever caress my nostrils at the thought of that moment. A drift of ground black pepper too. "Remember to take the cap off!" Daisy uttered as she deposited one of the larger ones between her dentures. From my earlier study of winkles, I knew what she meant. Numbed hands as they were, a right thumb and fore finger divined one of those escargots of the deep. I decapped-tated it, posted it in my oral orifice and chomped. 'Tough Heaven' was my innermost thought. My jaws clenched and relaxed, clenched again, as they do when chewing. But, for a seven year old, with eyes larger than his tum, this was a mouthful indeed. You know when you've taken a far too big bite of an apple, and you try to revolve it in your mouth and chew. Imagine that with a whelk! I was masticating as best as I could, (considering my age), that saline, gorgeous gelatinous hermit, slowly being reduced to swallowable morsels 'twixt tongue, gums and palate. This is when Daisy, after her third, said "Andrew, dear, have another" as she passed me the smallest. That was the moment when I choked. Then I coughed. Then I sneezed – chewed remnants of whelk left my closed mouth and somehow, as a baked bean has been known to do, entered my nasal passages, the ensuing sneezes scattered those tit-bits back to the 'Sussex Times' from whence they originated. Daisy deftly removed the sheet of grease proof with the remaining marine victuals as I sneezed yet again.

We were so relieved that those last whelks were removed and protected from that storm which I initiated, because the new contents of the 'Sussex Times' were virtually indistinguishable from the former. We took an open topped bus back to Brighton. The conductor wouldn't face the rain and wind, which was now assailing us, to collect our fares (an old ruse of Daisy's). I had another thrust at the last whelk, a small piece of newsprint adhering to its tail. It descended into my entrails with ease, the paper rested on my lip, to dry unnoticeably, in the wind as the weather changed and the conductor forgot us.

My college days were in London. Sir John Cass College in Aldgate. "Adgate East, Auld Get Out." As the Underground announcer would say (and then chuckle.) We got so bored with it! But... if I took a sharp right from the station and went past Blooms Restaurant, I reached Tubby Isaacs shellfish barrow. At this Haven, at the bottom end of Brick Lane, I could get, for a tanner, a gross amount of whelks, peppered, vinegarred, then chewed, (I had grown up by then so masticating was less of a chore,) they became a very satisfying late breakfast. My College friends were not initiated enough to become so ecstatic as I was about whelks, so, sometimes they refused an offering from the 'East End Gazette' and greaseproof bag, much to my delight.

More years elapsed, in fact many. I had been in Orkney potting away, oblivious to whelkzzzzzzzz. I was going to meet Sigrid, who was mounting an exhibition at her Black Pig Gallery in Victoria Street. I parked behind Bruce's Stores. A pick-up truck with red and blue plastic baskets was just drawing away. I spied the contents of those receptacles. WhelKKKKKKKKzzz, and what whoppers too. I got in front of that vehicle, flagged down its driver with an urgent jest of my hand. PHEW!! I was able to relieve him of a whole basket of those individuals. I rushed them to The Black Pig, where Sigrid was making her finishing touches. "Whelkx" I exclaimed, "we are so, so lucky. We can dine for weeks." Sigrid was not engendered with enthusiasm. The Opening of the show; Bob Shaw's etchings; what an array, what wit and talent in those pictures. Carlton Hill, pub scenes, a Spanish lady smoking; interiors with so many characters etched into copper and pressed to paper.

A quiet moment, and this is when my sweetheart discerned a scraping sound. She investigated her bijou, dinkie kitchenette, there, lo and behold were my giant whelks making for the sea. Their proboscises divining their route, their tails pointing inland, noses ocean ward. Crunch, scrape, and clatter they went as they made beach wards over the rim of their prison. I won't say that I was 'Ticked Off', but the incident has only just now been gotten over. You see 'fight ire with fire'.

I purchased a demi kilo of Boulots (French for whelks) boiled, sliced and set in a little mayonnaise dressing and a few wee herbs, they are as delicate as lambs' tongues.

Thanks for reading this ... Andrew

20 Sprogs

*'I never realised until years later how important this was.
From a sorry end for one sparrow, I was being tuned
in to nearly 180 years of stories of my forebears. '*

The chirping of a sparrow in the early a.m. is such a sound of delight, but by about 4.15pm, that morning pleasure is sometimes forgotten. This happened to me when I was about eight yearzez young. In our front garden, under the branches of our tall beech tree, deliciously light shootings of spring green leaves had just emerged from their buds. This forced a slow, shiny, scaly, brown drift of husks to our "lawn". Well! It was there that I was practising my aim with my first ever catapult. I looked up into that afore mentioned arbre and spied a mute sparrow hopping from twig to twig. That poor little bird was totally unaware that it had unwittingly become a target. A wee pebble extracted from our road metalling was secretly loaded into the leather pouch of my catapult. A long stretch of that wicked elastic and ... thwack!! ... sprog's end!

I couldn't believe it! There it was, giving a last flutter as its tiny wings drooped and movement ceased on our turf. I felt shocked and sorry, as well as pleased that my aim was so good, but I think that Late Sparrow probably hopped into the fatal pebble's trajectory, because I never hit anything else again (Sorry! Not true, there was that milk bottle). Anyway, 'Waste not your whatnot' was our family motto – amongst so many others – so, the now non-moving target, was taken to the place of preparation, namely our back doorstep.

The PLUCKING:
(Just as a hen or partridge), it had to be done without breaking the skin. Here, I discovered that plucking a bird still with the warmth of life within it was 'Très Facile' indeed. The pockmarks of my demi de-

feathered trophy's breast showed uniformly in a lined pattern. Soonly enough that design on its naked skin continued to the wings, neck, drum-twigs and parson's pimple. When denuded of plumage, that tiny carcase had to be singed. Holding its scaly toes and petite beak, it was revolved over a light blue London Gas flame. My fingers were not burned as this delicate process was coolly executed % ... (The scent of singeing any bird is a true kitchen smell. 100%-) ...%

The EVICERATION:

Tiny bird and my growing fingers!? Answer = Uncle Jerry's Japanese ivory chopsticks $$$. (My now dead American aunt, Juliet, used to wear chopsticks in her hair). That aside I delved into the oaken sideboard. There in their special lacquered case were those precious implements, en plus, – a long sharp steel mini Samourai dirk. The dirk severed the department twixt 'Parson's Pimple' and digestive organs. That passage, so created, the chopsticks were fingered with a swiftly learned dexterity. A deep push, several twists and her entrails entwined themselves on to those 'tuskan' treasures of the Orient. Duly extracted with a sharp lurch, GiZZarD and heart too appeared from within.

(HearTz To Follow, and GyzzUdZ.)

For TO COOK:

Nanna, our other Grand Mamma, was living with us then. She was 87 or so (in the shade). Our 'Front Room' became her 'Habitation'; Central to her East wall, her Hearth lay. There, hot coals glowed. Could her chambre fire become my cook spot? I knocked, then entered. Nanna was reading a 'Penny Novelette'. Whenever she came to a very big word that she couldn't get the meaning of, she said out loud "LONDON BRIDGE". There were many 'London Bridges' issuing forth. I interrupted her concentration with a request to barbecue my little sparrow on her fire. She blessed me by offering one of her long, thick knitting needles as a skewer for which to turn

it on, and a little cotton to secure the sparrow's legs tight to its revolving pinion. Thus secured, morsel of hedgerow assumed 'roasting position'. Nanna 'London Bridged' on.

A little time elapsed, as it does, ex-avian comestible rotated, an aroma dispersed. Nanna ceased 'London Bridging' and a soft, wet weeping came from her. I looked up to her from the grate and asked her, "Nanna. is Sparrow

Roasting upsetting you?" "No," she responded, "it just brings so many distant memories back." I removed warming dead dicky from the heat. "What memories, Nanna?"

She began. "My father, your great grandfather, was the son of a family butchers in Lewisham. When his father died (Nanna couldn't remember his name, but mentioned Lord Nelson and his fleet's supplies) my dad took over the shop." She continued, "When I was very young we went all around the fields of Lewisham together, Pepe's Hill and New Cross. In the evenings we took nets around the hedgerows. I beat one side of the hedge as he netted disturbed roosting sparrows on the other. We would take them home. He and mother would pluck them and prepare them for spit roasting over charcoal the next morning. Papa would get up awfully early and sell them to a stall, which barbecued them and sold them hot for posh folks breakfasts. A little bacon between each sproggy, and they were marvellous!".

I went to the 'Easy Work Cupboard' where rhind offcuts were jealously hoarded. Two horny bits were impaled either side of sprog, and she was replaced over the coals. I heard so much about South London in the 19th century, and with Nanna's tales of her parents and snippets of grandparents, I, by her fireside, was listening to handed history going back into the 18th century. I never realised until years later how important this was. From a sorry end for one sparrow, I was being tuned in to nearly 180 years of stories of my forebears. No wonder Nanny, or Lottie Stokes, née Reiman had a sentimental tear to shed — I would.

We shared that sparrow, nibbling every fibre of the breast, a leg each, a wing to pick at, a heart to share. The flavour was exquisite. I will never taste that again. A memory stored.

The sparrow in southern Britain is now almost a rarity. The swarms of them that used to be are diminished to a 'peppering'. They have been assaulted by petrol and diesel fumes; I am told that emissions from unleaded petrol cause infertility in these dickies. The absence of draft horses with spillings from their nose-bags has forced the 'Cockney Sparra' into the country, where it perishes for lack of wherewithals too. We are fortunate in Orkney, for we do still have havens for these tiny 'Brave Hearts'. My brother Stuart, in Grimeston, supports a small colony of them. At the Pottery we have a garden giving cover for Sparrows. In Stromness we still see a plethora of sprogs hopping in the street, pecking a dropped chip or some lost batter. Shopping Week is a bonanza time for them too, cleaning up burger droppings. After a flour delivery at Argo's Bakery, beaks are busy.

Lets all make an effort to retain our feathery chums, whose A.M. Chorus brings joy and cheer. Support that Sparrow family and allow it to grow, lest the chorus becometh a 'solo'.

Yours Aye, Andrew

Lottie Stokes (Nanna)

21 Healthy drinking

'You may have heard of my huge shopping basket on wheels, which I take to market. It is the 'Rolls Royce' of wheelie bags. Other shoppers gaze, then examine its undercarriage and stand back in wonder.'

Dear reader, if you are still there, Sigrid and I have so far spent an ailment-less winter. I don't know whether you have? We've had small injuries, like a poisoned finger due to a stab from a thorn, or scorch on a hand whilst muir burning. But nothing like 'Phflugh'. In France we call this 'La Grippe' – friends of ours have been laid waste to it. Jerome, the sculptor, who works with us from time to time, had to flee awa back home to his bed with some sort of gastric phenomenon which was running rife in the villages around. There were headlines in the 'Orkney Today' of Lot, otherwise known here as 'La Dépêche' splash headlined 'Pandémie de Grippe!' Even the poor lady in the Pottery Shop had it, no 'Bisou' from her, (or, was it just an excuse?).

So, there were lots of ill people all around. We were not sure why we were not ill too!! Then we thought back to our dear friends, David and Tina Hodge. Their combined ages assume quite a goodly count, but they always look so fit and healthy. David is the eminent silversmith on Burray who taught at Gray's School of Art, Aberdeen. One of his prodiges is none other than our very own Ola Gorie. Also highly esteemed. Well! Tina has her special talents too. A great sense of cultural ambiance flows through their home. Baking of the most delicious quality, delightful conversation and wit. It was during one of those perfect visits when we asked: "Tina, how do you do it!? Keeping so youthful and healthy!? The both of you?"

Tina thought then said: " Well, you know, Andrew, David and I started to eat Ginger. We found out about it in China, and now we have it every day." "Raw?" we asked. "Well, mostly" Tina replied. I didn't like the thought of it too much, raw ginger! We like chocolate gingers, ginger bickies, and sometimes candied ginger, but this seemed really too un-diet-like for us, so we forgot about it. (Well, not quite, actually).

We were at dinner with other friends, and Stephane had made a grated carrot and ginger salad. It was brilliant! We began to think again about this root. (Not that carrot though) "Heath, HEALTH, HealtH" were the thoughts for us. My new year's resolution was not to give up something as that is NEGATIVE. No, Andrew, take up something POSITIVE. So, we did. It was GINGER. We had to find some way of having it every day in a raw state that was palatable for us. If you delay, you forget, so it was an early morning thing for us.

Martyr me, is usually up first (Not really Martyr, simply bladder control). Then I put the kettle on for tea. I get so bored waiting for kettles to simmer, let alone boil, so I had to DO something. I reached for the ginger root. I grated some of it; I squeezed a lemon and shared the juice between our cups, a spoonful of honey in each. The water boiled. I poured – it all mixed and melded – I creaked upstairs, a cup supported by each thumb and palm.

Sigrid snoozed so sweetly as I placed her libation aside her pillow. I eased a curtain, a left and then her right eyelid, fluttered. A hand divined the cup. My presence of mind alerted me to the possibility of ensuing shock of 'UN Tea'. I, therefore, explained softly to Min Elskling "This is NEW Health drink." I surely spared her that shock. Amazingly it was even very palatable!! The hot water had reduced the strong taste of the ginger, all its essences were in that unguent, and the honey was a sweetener against that lemon. It has now become our every morning 'Health Drink' which we enjoy so mutchly. It is still a firm ritual. Thanks to D and T.

We do, however, have another ritual, which I shall tell you all about. It concerns the bottle bank. You may have heard of my huge shopping basket on wheels, which I take to market. It is the 'Rolls Royce' of wheelie bags. Other shoppers gaze, then examine its

undercarriage and stand back in wonder. Well! This 'Cart' of mine bides in our back lobby, you know, that dark bit where you store stuff that you pretend you don't really own. Cartie lives there all week. Cartie has become the receptacle for all the glass containers to be deposited in the 'Bottle Bank'. Our Saturday, en-route to market, ritual is to stop with 'Cartie' at Bottle Bank, by our bubbling brook and invest these very verres there.

This is how the 'Ritual' goes – Pick out the first bottle, call out loudly what it is ###. An Example: "WINE!" The next bottle has to be "Un wine" and definitely not alcoholic. "MUSTARD!" Then we are even. The following flask to be crashed has to be (if there are any left) something of the 'Beverage' variety. "Noilly Prat!" Then you nod and say: "That lasted Sigrid a long while." We come to the next victim – another innocent has to be removed. "TOMATO JUICE!" That is fine, it is in the rules. It is another of Andrew's Health drinks. In the bin – evens again. Go for beer. "Beer!" one shouts "Worcestershire Sauce." Quits! "Grouse!" "Mayonnaise!" Eye to eye again. (This is getting tense now.) "Chablis." "Pickled onions?" Close one that!! There could have been a wee bit of alcohol in the vinegar, but the Umpires missed it. "Pastis!" (That's been around forever). "Juice!" Neck and neck! "Wine.""Mustard." Close one there. "Beer" that was Godfrey, "Patè jar". Neighbour's gift.

Next set. "Gordon's Gin." "Litre Tonic." Close one. "Angostura bitters" – F A U L T T !! "Angostura is non-alcoholic so 'advantage'. "FRUITIES." "Light bulb." "Net!" – Light bulbs are vacuums, therefore not applicable. "DIEUCE." "Juice!" Umpire says: "Swift one there, but Alcohol to serve ... nil points." "Champagne." $$ "Lucozade!" Cans all, and then love. "Armagnac." "Perrier." >> match point. Alcohol serves with "SCAPA" ... Non alcohol has nothing left! That light bulb was the last chance. The bit of broken mirror doesn't count cither, so can't serve it! "WAAAH!!" – Health WILL lose ... But Lo! There, reflected in the darkest corner of that stalwart carrier, by the lonely chip of reflective glass, a wee dark brown flask, match point, yes!! HOOORRAYE!!! "BABY BIO" AHA!! Health are the champions, Health are the champions!! PHEW!!!

"NEXT." Off now to buy root ginger, honey and lemons at the market.

Yourzaye Andiroo and Sigiroo.

22 Goujon nights

'It's like anything, I suppose, you just have to get used to it; rough with the smooth, hard with the soft, reel on regardless. So we did. It became one of those absolutely special evenings.'

Fishing is one of those things that I have so little time for now. It takes a lot of planning to win that few hours. It is a shame because I enjoy it so. My brother Stuart is a great one for tying flies. His artistry is astounding. In much earlier days we used to make our own rods. Mine were from a hazel brand, or maybe a stout willow frond. Stuart made split cane ones and then early fibreglass rods. Hollow fibreglass was a favourite of his for lightness and strength.

I was usually looked down upon at the lakes and ponds because of the 'Rustic Nature' of my equipment. However, I always thought that it was 'what was in the water' that counted and not what was out of it! We nearly always caught fish, even on the bad days. We would go to 'private' waters where it was only 'club fishing'. Other anglers would look pityingly at us and allow us to stay. A few casts of my reel-less rod and my little hook would have a Rud or a Roach landed. These I sold for 'live bait' to those luckless, over tackled, ones that patiently lined the bank.

A bit of silver paper from a Woodbines packet on my tiny barb would attract the attention of a Perch. They were quite tasty, if a little sweet. In streams we'd stir up muddy bits and catch Gudgeon on a

feeding frenzy. In batter these fingerlings could be delicious, but watch your tongue, they were very hot straight from the chip pan. Gudgeon have thus given their name (and lives) to the, now ubiquitous GOUJON. You get goujons of 'tender chicken'. Pork Gougons in tangy rice, fisherman's platter with seafood gougons. Little ****** goujons everywhere. One reason for the original gougon is that the tender gudgeon has a propensity to fall apart when cooking, just like whitebait. That's why they are coated in flour or batter. When you next see that 'goujon' on the menu you can take it with a pinch of salt now.

Once every twenty-two years I go fishing with Angus McDonald of Merkister fame. I wasn't embarrassed at all with my "tackle" Schoolboy rod, wooden reel, a jar of worms, odd wellies. He said: "You're nay coming in me boat wi' that."

I replied that it was too late, as I was already in. Angus nursed a frown. His engine spluttered and we went right out of sight of the hotel, as far away as he could get me, lest anybody had a telephoto lens fixed on us.

My fisherman friend cast to the right and left, with the wind and without it. He saw plenty of rises, but no fish touching. I was yet to learn the art of the fly, so I flayed the brandling. A little too 'fresh' I remarked when my worm parted from its heid. As Angus changed flies, I plied wriggling 'mustard'. Angus cast again. No joy. Me neither. Angus did "Tut" at me as wormz isn't "Proper" (and still aren't.) We persevered, him with an "I Don't Ken Wot" and me with a big, fat lobworm. I suppose that digging for worms can be more exciting than fishing, as each worm represents a chance. Each fly tied, too gives the same ambition. It is when you're in the boat when it's 'Face The Music Time' and it's what's in the water and not above it that counts. Angus cast, I lobbed. Fish took my worm. Angus cleared his throat: "How did you manage that with ***** tackle?" "Magic" was all I needed to report. What I think was so cruel of me, was, at the next instant I said: "Angus! Your fish is my command!!" I then pointed to the waters and said: "Strike!" He did... and there... on the end of his line... hooked sportingly... was a beauty.

We had a lovely afternoon on the Loch. I didn't want to catch any more, so I didn't. I dapped a few times and maybe trailed a worm behind the boat, but I made sure I didn't catch anything else. My sole fish was all I needed. Angus's wize saying was "A day on the loch is not counted as a day off your life." I hope sharing that time with me wasn't counted against him.

Strangely enough, another 22 years has nearly elapsed. Will I be spared to share another afternoon with Angus? Whaa kens?

* * * * *

My latest fishing trip was with Sigrid and my brother Stuart, friend

Simon O'Heddle, and Dave O' The Chess Club came too; then Dave "Fell Asleep" at the first big wave. We were out with Alistair of Out West Charters. He does sea-fishing trips from Stromness in the evenings. (850 621) This was my second trip with him in a month, but then I wasn't using my "Tackle" He supplies tackle for the needy, like me. Stuart was all beautifully tackled up to the hilt though, well, he's a proper fisherman.

Alistair "drove" us out to sea. It was so beautiful. We went oer Graemsay Sound and then further out to below St. John's Head. It was fabulous to be in such surroundings. Sea birds flapping about everywhere, posh gulls, sea gulls, ordinary gulls, guillemots (I know them). The colours of the water and the sandstone cliffs; it was worth the hire just for this alone.

We were taken to one of his favourite drifts. Here, he said we would get mackerel; he cut the engine and we feathered our lines. This was the stuff for Sigrid, a real seagoing Dane. Stuart was in his element, and Dave had scored 9 on the vomitometer. Lines were lowered, no need for casting. Down, down, down they went, and then wiggle, wiggle, wiggle, that was the feeling on the end in the depths. A sharp tug, and the reeling in commenced. It was then that I wished there was only one "Down" and not three, as I mentioned earlier. It was HARD WORK reeling and reeling. Simon was very good at it though, he could reel awfully well. I asked Alistair if there was a machine for this. He said: "Yes! – It's called a trawler" I continued this reeling action, as we all did, including Dave in his very special way.

Plenty of mackerel now, so we moved on to "coddy" waters. Stopping again to drift we could see a September full moon rising and reflecting on the sea. Mackerel baited hooks went below to those saline depths. Fish eyes, noses and sensors recorded the presence of GRUB. They approached, and TUG, Tug, tuggle. A fishie!! Hauling them up was even harder. Stuart was working away at a big fish as strange things were happening on the end of my line. What a weight was on there. At last, out from the waters surfaced a Pollack for me.

Alistair took it off my hook, turned his head and said "Too small" and chucked it straight back.

All that work had to start all over again. Dave was Moon Gazing. It's like anything, I suppose, you just have to get used to it; rough with the smooth, hard with the soft, reel on regardless. So we did. It became one of those absolutely special evenings. We did get cod, quite enough for us;

we had pollack too and loads of mackerel. We sailed back towards Hamnavoe, tired, cool and happy. Dave had perked up and said he'd really enjoyed watching us catch fish for him. He took his share back to Mithist and Simon took Stuart back to Grimeston, but not before something "warming" at home in the form of freshly grilled mackerel and Argo's crusty bread to mop up those juices.

Yourzaye, Andrew.

P.S. Sigrid was relieved not to have caught a single fishie at all ````S

'The Goujon Knights'

23 Grooved Ware Pottery

*'Pattern and design always has to be
based on something, and mostly it is based
on what you see on a daily basis.'*

The Grooved ware Pottery which was found at Skara Brae has interested me for a number of years. Let me describe it to you. Firstly, there were vast vats created from the very poor Orkney clay. Some of these vessels were certainly nearly a meter high and just as broad. This is potting on a grand scale. The decoration is just as bold as the pots it adorned.

There were platters made from a more refined clay, these were burnished smoothly and will have shone when new. Finely made beakers with a reddened surface, rougher cooking pots, flat bowls, dishes and urns.

Sigrid and I were to spend some time in Edinburgh and we felt that this would provide a fine opportunity to examine the wares from Skara Brae at first hand. We had visited Glasgow University a few years before and studied the Crossie Crown Grooved Ware from that Neolithic Village, so it would be good to compare it.

We were very fortunate in getting special permission from Trevor Cowie of The National Museum Of Scotland to look through the finds from Professor Childe's excavations. These were carried out way back in the 1930's. This collection is wrapped in tissue paper  with each group of sherds in its own designated poly bag. There is also the carefully typed book of Childe's with a description of these groups. Everything is numbered and this correlates with digits written on the bits of pot. Jim, the store-man, prepared everything for us. Sigrid and I were left free to examine and make notes, do drawings and take photographs.

I have experimented with some of the clays from around Skaill Bay. I can tell you that it is terrible to work with. It is full of rocks and rubble; typical glacial till. It is decidedly un-plastic. When you try to build pots with it the clay goes all floppy and sags. This is because of the high sand and decayed rock content. Imagine firm beach sand, then, vibrate it; it goes all soft and runny. This is what happens to Skaill clay. Of course, the Neolithic inhabitants knew their environment far better than I do; also the landscape there has changed dramatically over the past millennia. Perhaps their clay source has been covered by dunes, or even washed away by erosion, I don't know.

We began to unwrap the sherds. No complete pot has come from Skara Brae, but that's ok, you can in fact tell more about a pot from its broken remains. It is those huge vats, which intrigued us so much. The sections of the sherds clearly showed the extremely rough 'core' of the pots. Great lumps of stone and grit were all the way through it. Over this inner core, a layer of finer clay had been spread. This clay will have been prepared by making rough clay into a liquid, perhaps in a pit, allowed to settle and then the finer 'levigated' clay removed from the top. Then the decoration could be applied. After the decoration had firmed up, a further, even finer, coat of liquid clay was painted all over the surface. This sealed the decoration and strengthened it.

This design work has been judged as 'pattern'. There are horizontal strips of clay applied to the pots, some creating bands a few inches under the great rims. Striking out from these bands, bold triangular zones appear. These are 'mirrored' by others below. Sometimes there are applied 'pellets' of clay filling these zones. Often there is an impressed groove on the bands and sometimes either side too. These grooves cast a wee shadow and give definition to the design.

When you look at that 'pattern'. and store it in your brain, you recognise it instantly when you observe Orkney's landscape. On a bonny day you see this decoration as the hills reflect in the lochs. It is stunning to visualise it like this. It leaves such a strong impression. I have tried to convince myself that it is just 'pattern' on those vats, but the more Sigrid and I look at those pots, the more they look back at us. Pattern and design always has to be based on something, and mostly it is based on what you see on a daily basis. Was this Orkney being depicted on pots? I rather think so!

The structure of 'Grooved Ware' decoration is largely based on straight lines. These straight lines can form triangles, lozenges and slanted raised zones. It is rare to get curves, circles or spirals. Only one shard with spirals is known to exist from Skara Brae. It is a famous piece and has inspired jewellers and print makers from Orkney. Much has been written about it, but it is not typical at all.

As this pottery is now nudging 5,000 years old, it is distinctly friable. The decoration has dropped off in places, leaving the under surface exposed. Here is where some of its secrets lie. One shard, HA 226, very faint lines made by the potter who marked out the decoration, can only just be seen, but they are there! We even saw where some of the "Pellets" had fallen away on that special piece. It was special in several ways. The positions of the pellets had been marked with a tiny impressed dot from a pin. The remaining pellets had the tiniest of finger-marks on them. Only a bairn could have squeezed those pellets on, and there was Mum or Dad's mark to guide that little him or her. (Was this an earlier Madonna and Childe?) The rim of this pot was beautifully decorated too. It resembled the way I inter-fit mussel shells as I eat them, thus forming a pattern round my plate. Were they playing with their mussel shells too? I don't see why not. It was this experience that gave us one of those specially rare archaeological thrills. There were more to come.

Fifteen years previous to our recent visit, I was at the, then Royal Museum Of Scotland. Andrew Foxon took me to the stores and showed me a group of Childe's sherds. He asked me what I made of them. They were a puzzle to him as they had curved, almost arched, applied stripes. I could not interpret that decoration at all. So we chatted about other pots in general. These same sherds were in front of Sigrid and me for a second time!

Only ten years before this, I had been looking at some of the carved stones in the little old museum at Skara Brae. There was a "Pattern" which I was intrigued with. I took a tracing of it. A few days later it dawned on me when I looked at it the other way round, that it was a "Landscape Picture". It was the ancient Neolithic view from Skara Brae to Scotland. Of course, in those days there was a

sandbar in front of the village, which held back a large area of brackish water. This stone showed those mountains of Sutherland sticking out and up behind that sandbar. The water was shown by almost parallel diminishing triangles. This gave an excellent effect of perspective. I published this discovery, it has been disputed, but generally, now, it is accepted as a picture showing the shallow loch with the now vanished dune.

Back to Andrew Foxon's fragments; sherds HA 228-229-230; another huge vat. The arched lines were still there, utterly bold. We could tell by the way the pot was made which way up this decoration was. There were almost lozenge-shaped protrusions coming from these arches with rough pin impressions in the middle of them. I was looking too hard. Sigrid was behind me and said: "Oooh! Look Andrew, they are leaves." I looked and thought: "No, can't be" I thought this because nobody has found applied leaves on Neolithic pottery before, well not in the U.K. I removed my "dogmatic hat" We looked again. They really did appear to be leaves. It was a shock. Our spines tingled. You see, it is like seeing something for the first time; something which has been totally overlooked and miss-interpreted.

Sigrid and I can look at ancient pottery and visualise it in its new state; polished, burnished, in use. This is because we do remake pots of the past, using the genuine techniques of the day. It is then that you see the "Real Thing" especially if you use it as it was used.

Sherd HA229 was under scrutiny. Childe's description said something like "Applied smudged pellet of clay" I was trying to draw it when Sigrid said "Gosh! Andrew, that's a birds head." "Can't be" was my reaction. Then I looked the way Sigrid was looking, with an open eye, rather than a blinkered one. I nodded, "Bird's Head" We looked closer; there, where the beak is, a very faint line showed the opening of the bill. The vestige of a dot was in the correct position of the eye. This was yet another spine tingling moment. It was only the head and a bit of neck. What kind of bird? Certainly a seabird, and it was "underneath the arches"

That was quite enough for one day. We had seen so much.

We returned to Keith and Laure's house, where we were staying. We had been discussing dickie birds or the marine varieties thereof, and hadn't come up with much. We thought "Gannet." But it didn't seem right. We felt that a bird of great esteem would have been depicted. Albert Ross came to mind. Then we discussed a little further. That pot was made perhaps 5,000 years ago; has that bird vanished from Scotland and Orkney? Spine chill factor at 100 percent hit us! Was it the extinct Great Auk? We went to Keith's bird book and looked up 'Great Auk' it wasn't there. Then we tried 'Auk' and found 'Auk, Great'

We turned to the designated pages, and there was an old illustration of one. It matched exactly our 'Auk' shard.

Our bird was being depicted in amongst flora. What flora? A Great seabird in a flowerbed? Not really, but could it be the Loch in front of the Skara Brae Village that we are seeing? Certainly these are extra ordinary sherds. Is this foliage from reed like plants? If this is a Great Auk, are we seeing it in the middle distance, or through the reeds? We find the whole aspect of this startling.

Great Auk bones have been recovered from excavations at Skara Brae, I am told. I think it very reasonable for the waters facing Skara Brae to be an ideal habitat for a colony of those flightless birds. The loch would provide ideal breeding conditions for such a colony. If we are right, and I think we are, then there is a case for this grooved ware pottery to be examined in a new light from which it has been in the past. It could also show how Orkney's ancient potters were making things in quite a different way than elsewhere, thus revealing different traditions.

I applied for a grant to carry out further research on this. I was fortunate to be assisted by HI~ATRS, though other approaches failed. Whilst waiting for the "no" answer we decided to do a little preparation in advance of "The Big Experiment." This was to re-make a selection of these pieces in their traditional forms, using the means available to the Neolithic potter. We only used elements of decoration that we found on the pots. Sigrid and I wanted to see just what these things were like when new, and show you too. We think the accompanying photographs will demonstrate just that.

There is so much more to do on this subject. If we are really to understand Orkney's Neolithic, then re-creating these things is an integral part of that process. Sherds and bits don't tell the whole story. They are only part of it, giving us clues, which we now can follow up to such a great extent, if given the resources.

PS. Since this was first published in 'Orkney Today', Eric Meek, our professional bird expert has spotted a Dunter Duck's head lurking

in the reeds on the pottery. He absolutely confirms the 'smudged pellet of clay' is indeed the head of the Great Auk. So too does his fiel assistant, Aileen Hall. Julia Robinson-Dean also concurs with the Auk interpretation. Errol Fuller, author of the mighty tome 'The Great Auk', says that it can be nothing else but the Auk. He added that the depiction is the second oldest representation known to archaelogical science – the oldest being from a cave in the Pyrenees dated to 40,000 B.P.

An archeao-botanist from Oxford identified the 'leaves' as opening seed heads of a yellow flag. Apparently the seeds are rich in oils and nourishment.

So, with these crumbling shards, do we have yet another archaeological treasure from Orkney? I do think so, in fact Sigrid and I believe them to be of fundamental importance and they should be publicly and scholastically recognised. (I will shut up now, but never hold my peace.) A

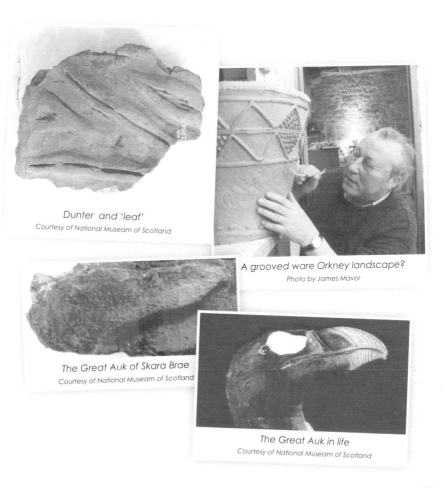

Dunter and 'leaf'
Courtesy of National Museum of Scotland

A grooved ware Orkney landscape?
Photo by James Mavor

The Great Auk of Skara Brae
Courtesy of National Museum of Scotland

The Great Auk in life
Courtesy of National Museum of Scotland

24 Eels

'"Why did no-one tell me of this before!!"
This "Deep Secret" hath been kept too long.'

The other Friday, Sigrid and I called in at Jollies to pick up our specially smoked salmon. Brian had heard from the 'boys' that I had been pleading and pleading for a carcase of that 'King of Fish', the Conger eel. I say 'King' because 'Konge' is the Danish word for King and properly prepared and cooked, this marine beast is an utter favourite of mine. We can buy great tranches of them in our market in France, but it is not cheap! The closer you get to the head, the better the flesh. In fact the head of a Conger makes a fabulous stock for a fishy soup. Boil that heeid, crown and all, strain the stock, remove slippery skin, flake the gentle flesh off around the cheeks, and skin its little tongue. This is an easy task really, it just reads as gruesome. Return conger flesh to the stock, fling in diced tatties; stir fry a finely chopped leek. When tatties are nearly cooked, sling in a handful of prawns, then the leek. Dump a bit of Crantit cream in and stir; season and herb to taste. Dish out. Just grand!!

Another favourite mode of turning those thick conger steaks into a splendid repast is to warm an oven dish and soften some butter in it. Float in that warm runny liquid, some sliced shallots or onion. Place your 'royal' fish portions into that butter, turn them over, sprinkle

with salt, pepper and some capers, maybe diced red pepper too, then add some milk. Cover dish with foil and cook gently. When the milk hath evaporated some, remove the foil and allow a little yellowing and browning to occur, then it's ready.

This dish is excellent served with creamed tatties. If you have mange tout peas, shove a few per person on the plates and serve the eel and sauce from the dish over them, for they will be bright, warm and crunchy. As you place that first fork full of soft, gentle, pure, white, Royal Marine flesh into your gob, you will be amazed. The wonder, the texture of this brave of the deep will caress your tongue. You will cry out: "Why did no-one tell me of this before!!" This "Deep Secret" hath been kept too long. Go to Jollies, speer for that fish culled wonder, cook and enjoy.

I had to take my 21-kilo eel down to Stromness pier for gutting. I washed it a bit, then, took it up home where I sliced it into convenient portions. This was made easy because I borrowed a couple of really, really sharp knives from Fletts Butchers. That eel now rests deep frozen, awaiting the appointed hour for the heeid to be removed, or a thick 'Shoulder Steak' for thawing. If you are worried about this whole process, I am sure all the Jolly boys will do the dirty work for you.

My eel fetish began when I was eleven. Dad had this sudden urge to take us to Rye in East Sussex to catch some of these slimeys. If we got our skates on, we could be at Bromley South Station and get a cheap return to that Cinq Port and catch the tide on the River Rother. We got that train. Rye loomed. We headed for the water's edge. The tide was out!! Mud flats everywhere. We went to the place nearest the water and we cast out our weighted, baited lines. Swish, splat! Ledger and lure lodged in mud! Dad got very excited as we put up a few snipe. He went on about how lucky we were to see them. "A common birdie in Orkney," he consoled, "but very rare indeed in the South of England." Malcolm asked if eels were common in Orkney too!? =+= Dad made no reply.

I was the smallest of the family. I had difficulty therefore in retrieving my tackle. Venturing forward on to the edge of the mud, which had a dry crust, I reeled in, or tried to. The line was shortening. The precious tackle was getting inexorably closer, however I noticed that it was me approaching the lurid morass and far from the reverse. I had advanced some feet on those crusty alluvial soles beneath my shoes. Behind me were the tracks of my Rotherward progress, sloping down. The strange effects of gravity would soon overcome any friction holding me to that spot. Mum and Dad were heading for the Harbour Side Café and Bar, when Malcolm realised the sheer levity, for him, incidentally, of my situation. His laughter attracted the attention of parting parents. Dad yelled: "Andrew, stop reeling in!" "Superfluous advice" I mused. I unleashed the ratchet on my wooden reel, turned at 98 degrees 43 seconds and pointed my rod tip to Malcolm. He twigged. Reaching for the top eye, which still had attached a desiccated lobworm from our last trip, he gripped it. I detected a slight push. I pulled, he gained on me, as he realised HIS peril, so he behaved. Mum reached over Malcolm and towed me back on my slippery path towards relative safety. As I skewed the remaining 91 degrees 57 seconds, my centre of balance altered, causing added pressure under my feet. My face met mud. But my rod, that very staff of life, was, however, closer to my kinsfolk. Even-handedly, they jerked me towards them, Mother saying "Andy, dear, don't let go" – "As if?"

My hands were, amazingly, moderately clean, so I could be assisted up. I severed my nylon fishing line with a few sparks from father's 'Ronson' lighter. We sauntered bar-wards. I was not allowed into this hostelry funnily enough, so I was fed a few titbits outside and had to remain well away from the door. Malcolm joined me later, and we explored the harbour as white froth slowly evaporated from Dad's upper lip, that same froth descended the transparent sides of his glass several times. We peered down the harbour walls, and there, nosing out from the rocks was an eel greeting the rising tide. We returned to the 'scene of the grime' just as the snipes winged their way back to their muddy domain.

What a Rye experience we all had!!.

ANDREW

25 Hens

*'At night I would go to her shed and hold her when she
was perching. I could brave the darkness for her.'*

It is very pleasant to wait for the Hamnavoe in the tea lounge of
the Pentland Hotel in Thurso. It certainly outstrips the waiting
room at the Scrabster Terminal. I have a lovely electric plug here
for 'Monty' my laptop, where there is no such facility at the Docks.

The waitress has just taken an order for three "Chicken in the
Basket" and a "Scampi Platter." Doesn't it bring it all back to you?
Anyway, my intro is over. It just reminds me of Hetty. She was my
hen and faithful friend. When I was two and a half-and-a-bit, she
was a frighteningly big black and white speckled hen. As I grew, she
seemed to get weeer. I think we reached equilibrium when I was six
and not a lot more.

I overcame the fear of this hen when she had chicks, one got left
behind in the rain, and was getting cold. I wanted to bring the chick
in and warm it in the oven and "Rescue" it. Dad said that I must leave
it to nature as the hen would come back for it. Hetty didn't return,
poor hen, she couldn't count. The darkening sky matched the mood
in my heart. I watched through the curtains of the French windows
as the nine-day-old fledgling keeled over. I ran out, hearing dad calling
"Shut the b***d*n' curtains, it's draughty".

Little me splashed out into our garden. The soaked plumage,
open beak and unblinking eye indicated 'curtains' for that perished
'poulet'. I wished at that moment that it was 'curtains' for a different
'critter'. Clutching that soaken corpse, I took it to Hetty, who was in
the covered run with all her other chicks. I told her that I was
very sorry indeed for not saving her poorly infant. She pecked
and scratched, teaching the remains of her brood the arts of

chickenhood. Life went on.

She was a good mum, so I took her special treats, dug worms for her and found woodlice under stones, which she relished. At night I would go to her shed and hold her when she was perching; I could brave the darkness for her. It was easy to leave the light of the house for the shadows of the garden to make my way to her coop. I had to round a corner beneath a rowan tree, there, it was even blacker. I would give Hetty a 'Pedicure'; her scaly feet gleaming in the pitch dark. I got the dry, rough bits out of her comb, bringing it back to red splendour, instead of 'Henny Penny Muddy' colour.

Little did I know about the plot which was thickening.

We collected Hetty's eggs. Each ovum had pencilled on its shell the initials of its recipient. Whether boiled, scrambled, fried or poached, this was the choice of that morning's breakfaster. One of those times, Mum said, "Andieroo, there's noo en egg for you." "Why not?" I queried.

Mother extrapolated thus – "Hetty's off the lay, and your father says that she's for the pot!" My Pater's reported speech did not have a blessed effect on me. Six, though I was, I mooted this point. "Hetty is my hen. This is Monday, she will lay again on Wednesday of next week, and a double yolker too."

I encouraged her with crushed oyster shells, cabbage stump (which she loved) boiled tattie skins with bran (couldn't afford layers mash) old tea slops and crusts. Hetty pecked, Hetty enjoyed, Hetty grew. I knew by her cluck that that bird was "With Egg". Hetty was on the point of lay. On the Tuesday morning, when we had porridge, I announced that Hetty will lay on Wednesday evening, tomorrow, indeed!!

I had a very lucky childhood; I was privileged to attend the Wickham Common County Primary School. (I oft didn't). On a Wednesday afternoon I helped the 'Rag and Bone Man'. That Wednesday I arrived back home at three thirty seven P.M. to see my Father and a Brother writhing in glee o'er the quivering corpse of Hetty. She had been ignominiously throttled to great injury of her neck, causing fear, trauma, and severely unjust early demise. Her

slowly beating wing and the glazed eye signalled her final curtain. I WAS BEREFT.

On the Friday, Mum plucked her; she had hung from the corrugated roofed garage. Mucus oozing from her suspended beak's nostrils. I was witness. That evening Mum and I gutted her. It had to be done. When we opened her we found a firm shell at the very point of nativity. My mother and I gently removed that egg. Following it by the strand were dozens of eggs, just queuing up to be placed before us. The first one we cracked, a double yolker it was. There were others. We saved them for baking and mayonnaise. We couldn't waste Hetty, could we!

After all my tears, I braved up. Sunday lunch, slow cooked hen. My family assembled at table. That dimpled yellow enamel casserole, her hot sarcophagus, was emplaced at my Father's setting. "Who wants what?" he asked. "Leg, wing, breast?" I called for "Parson's Nose, leg and wing" – all his favourites. My family thought I was being a greedy-guts. Dad said that, that just showed that I didn't care about Hetty one jot. I fairly let them ken that it was a far better thing that I scoffed as much of her as I could, so as to save her from their digestive tracts and farts.

Hetty's demise has been a bone of contention in our family ever since. I will not doubt that her flavour was of the utmost bliss. She rewarded me to the end. My innocent fattening of her in her last few days added to the essence. My family's guilt lies with those cakes, the batter and that salad dressing posthumously performed.

I am so partial, now, to genuine 'out of lay hen' that I visit Mrs Hepburn on a seasonal basis. She brings on her hens at Burnside, Tankerness. She loves her birds. She rears ducks, geese, turkeys, a bantie or three, and there are moorhens in the wilds of her burn. Sometimes she has "Cockie hens". What they are, I don't ken. I do ken that they are very edible. What kind Mrs Hepburn allows me are her old cockerels, ancient muvver hens and a few eggs for bye.

Her old fowl I sort. They stew in a pot for yonks. I can tell you that they are far better than any portion controlled convenience thing from easy freezy. They need time and care, love and tenderness, some carrots and a few onions, salt and pepper.

When I took this Photie of Mrs "H", I asked her the chuck's name, she said "Hettie" I said, "Release that hen!" That was a near death experience, which I could never have been an accomplice to.

Andrew

26 One flu over the chicken shed

'That first summer slipped by. the only thing I missed was runner beans. I advertised in 'The Orcadian' and folk posted these goodies to me from all parts sooth.'

Yesterday my daughter, Ruth, sent me one of my early pots that I had made 30 years ago at the Old Chicken House on Fursbreck Farm. This was the birthplace of my pottery in Orkney. In those days I hand signed my pieces 'Fursbreck Orkney'. One of Ruth's customers wants a set of my "Old" stuff. I shall comply as best as I can. Looking at this piece, though, brought back many memories of Grimeston.

My arrival there lent an unexpected tone of notoriety to the toonship, I don't know why. That first summer season saw 'TOURISTS' and visitors, inquisitors, cars, motorbikes and yes!!! Coaches came to this unsuspecting backwater of idyllic Orkney. They even risked negotiating the very narrow and rutted farm track to my obscure workshop at the back of the midden. I was advised by visiting "Business Experts" to set up in the City of Kirkwall. I was a country boy after all, so the Toon wasn't for me. I preferred to bide in the whins and brecks, dykes and fields.

Wherever you are, it is your neighbours that make your new territory 'home'. The Aim family, Peter and Joan with Jackie, their daughter and David, their son. He became, for a while, my very first E.C.L. (Exploited Child Labour) of the pottery. Caleb and Bell Walter of Nearhouse Farm with Willie and Mary Swannay, their "Fairm Servants" who bided at Nort House. Bella Feolquoy, and her man, Truthful Mack, who told stories of survival in the snowbound Grampian Mountains, with only a steam locomotive for shelter and comfort. Bella welcomed me and my brother Stuart heartily. She doned to me an old iron Army bed, from which I entertained several coach parties of local women's guilds and groups. (I had seriously hurt my back and was ordered "Bed Rest" by the veritable Dr. Black.) The Show had to go on, so it did. Those that witnessed these proceedings, like me, have a 'gem' for a memory.

That first summer slipped by. The only thing I missed was runner beans. I advertised in the 'Orcadian' and folk posted these goodies to me from all parts Sooth. Plain, brown wrapped packages with wobbly contents for Bobby the Postie to deliver. Each donor received a "Bean Pot". So, thus, Orkney became my Paradise. Living in this concrete block and asbestos roofed chicken shed, 54ft. by 26ft. of blissful space, I was as happy as a pig in muck.

Just after my first New Year in Orkney I went back to Kent to visit my Mum, Madge. We always got on well, and as she had not long lost Dad, I felt she needed her chin tickled. I stayed a week or so and then returned. I found a note in my kitchen; it read: 'DON'T VISIT ANYBODY AT ALL. WE ALL HAVE FLU. AT OUR BACK DOOR THERE IS A BOX WITH FULL INSTRUCTIONS. — PETER AND JOAN'. I went to their door, there was the very tin cist waiting for me with a stone on top. I eased open the lid of that metal receptacle. Lying on its slightly rusting base rested my 'Code of Practice'. It informed me to please feed the beasts in the byre, morning and evening. I was to be careful to do the morning feed after Rowan (Jim) had done the 'Dighting' (Shovelling the Shyte). Rowan was well and was not to be infected. I then was asked to do an evening feed. Rations were explained to me. Dribbles of molasses should be eased over the hay for extra nutrition. (A bit like our molasses on fried bread when we were kids, I thought).I'm not too good at reading recipes and getting them right. I did my best. The kye got a little too much hay and syrup. James Rowan of Fursbreck had to shovel more Shhh stuff than usual, and it was of an increased skittery consistency, due to the dark, glistening garnish, which was not easy to control the proportions thereof. To describe James D. Rowan, you might say that he was a Noel Coward figure in a boiler suit and flat cap. I did remember the hint about not getting behind the fifth beast down on the left. "For, she kicks an awful lot!" I canne mind me left from me right anyroads, so I just avoided all their rear ends. That was Rowan's toil anyway, and not mine. What I did do though was to talk to each beasty and try something original to utter. They did lots of heavy breathing back and looked at me as though I really meant something to them. I did, however, build up a special relationship with an un-named coo. I dubbed her Joyce. She reminded me so of Mrs. J. Grenfell of Trinian's fame. Her name stuck

I checked the 'Quality Street' tin on a daily basis. At that time I had no phone. This metal box became the Grimeston Oracle. The News was that Willie had succumbed to the lurgie. Would I do Near Hoose's beasties too? Rowan would clear the cesters, the kye would fill them. If I could fill the kye, everybody would be well employed. I charged those kye like there would be no tomorrow. It was Caleb's big, black boggling bull who I was wary of. I used a very long pitchfork to sustain him and made a fast exit from his solitary chamber. No idle chitchat with bullie.

Peter and Joan were "Mending". Rowan never got smitten. The Aims got back to their previous pace. I was able to relax from the 'Bovine Front' after a couple more days. In that time of flu a recipe for continued existence was put into place. It succeeded in halting contagion and worked well.

Maggie O' Langskaill broadcast via her own 'Grimeston Gazette'the daily doings, along her phone poles and lines. The Toonship came back to life to face the March gales. I got back to potting, and possibly made that little beaker which Ruth posted to me.

Yours, Aye, Andrew

P.S. Perhaps we may get a flu flown in to us. If so, maybe we should adopt the Grimeston Code in a tin Oracle box. A

27 Shirley's ashes

'Lo and behold, a little down river was a wee, ruinous jetty with a disused diesel pump for passing thirsty flotillas at its furthermost point. We ventured there. A squeeze past a part derelict workshop and along some sodden duckboards, the funeral procession slithered.'

My Aunt Shirley was different. We called her "Our Hippie Aunt". In the very early sixties she married a Sudanese man and promptly went to bide in his "tent". She was his first wife and bore him Rashid, his first son. Shirley didn't mind the other wives that came along, but she wanted to be put first at all times. This didn't quite happen, so before Rash was four, and thus becoming the sole property of his dad, Shirley decided to flee in the night with her little boy. The servants plotted with her and secured midnight transport across the dunes to an airfield. There was no ululating, only swift, fond tearful hugs and departure.

Shirley taught in West London, and brought Rash up on her own. There were stupid family problems here, like he'd eat with his fingers. He'd only scoff the meat and refuse the veg. He'd simply take all the best bits and not contemplate any gristle. There was war at family Sunday lunches. You don't get your pudding unless you've cleaned your plate. "Poor Shirl," they used to say.

After lunch Rash would do his crayoning on the beige carpets and not use any paper. He'd only draw silly things and no one could stop him. I really took to Rash! On Sunday evenings a family worthy would ring up and tell all about Shirley's visit for lunch, or a weekend's stay. It was always the same, "Why can't that little black bomber learn some bleedin manners? Aye?"

He never did, and I'm glad. He was only doing what a first-born son of a Sudanese dignitary would do. Table manners demanded that he ate with his right hand; he always chose the prime meat just as he was instructed to do. He was to enjoy the best and have puddings and sweetmeats without touching a roasted tattie or boiled sprout if he didn't wish to. After his repast he was encouraged to draw pictures on the sandy floor. Those servants of his pater's will have educated him in their traditional art, where his mother couldn't. (Poor Shirl)

When I was about eighteen, Shirley asked me where I would recommend for a joint holiday for her fellow teachers and friends. I told her to ring Dr. and Mrs. Firth of Westness House, Rousay. and spear for The Manse at Burnside. This she did, and booked it for the whole summer. I was stupidly too busy to join them. Shirley and Rashid, (his grandmother, Daisy, (nicknamed Beetroot} called him 'Radish').

To her dying day, and that I shall come to, Shirley extolled her Holiday on Rousay as the very best one ever. Radish does too. Dear Shirl had a large and open house in Chiswick (opposite 'Inspector Morse's' home) This place was a haven for foreign students, most of them doing political studies of some sort. Whenever I visited there were interesting people with discussions going on, Moroccans, Turks, Latvians, Estonians, Paraguayans, Poles, Slavs and A' Folk. Sudanese to-ed and fro-ed, as did Chinese and Javanese. She had a rich life with all these guests and friends.

Shirley spent some time with Sigrid and me in France. We had ten days together doing all sorts of things. We laid a couple of medieval tiled steps to our front door. We put the world to rights, had forced marches, "Shirl speed". She fitted us in between a visit to Tunis and staying with Aisha Gull and Hassan in Istanbul. At 77 this was Shirley's life. She admitted that she'd always been troubled with catarrh, but whilst staying with us, it had cleared up. Our village is called St. Germain du bel-Air, so our clear ether must have been the reason.

As a vehement non-smoker, she, and we were, stunned when shortly after her visit she was "Dognosed" with lung cancer. It was "Non aggressive" but there. It would probably grow later and doo for her in the end, but there was time. Shirley therefore decided to

throw a 'Birthday Party'. This was to be on the banks of the Thames. A wonderful August night, probably two hundred folk from A' Parts O' the Globe, and family attended. This was a 'Swan Song' – there were two or three more "Occasions" after, but this was the big one).

I promised to make her a funerary urn (as a gift.) I did. She got it a week or three before she shrugged off the mortal coil. Sigrid and I visited her in her house as she was dying. We took her a bunch of fresh mint, which she clasped and enjoyed. Rash was there of course, and so were several friends from across the waters, coming to bid a farewell to this great lady. As always, her house was a throng.

We were heading for France, and a few days later she was dead. Cremation at Mortlake Cemetery, then a Humanist funeral service in Kew Gardens followed by a fabulous wake at a splendid Ethnic restaurant. We couldn't go. We were giving a residential course on Prehistoric Pottery. The theme was Bronze Age burial urns. Apt in its way, and Shirley would have joined in if "spared".

Read just how things went down in the ash spreading in 'Shirley's Ashes, Part Two'.

SHIRLEY'S ASHES Part Two

It was the autumn of 2002 when Poor Shirl expired. There was a long family debate in April 2003. When would we spread the ashes? Valerie, Shirley's executor wanted a June date and this was decided on. It was right for most of her Turkish friends and good for some Dutch folk. Shirley's house was still available as a venue. A Sunday scattering was declared. I was free and able to go. Sigrid had to remain at the helm here at the pottery.

It meant flying down on the Saturday and home again on Monday. I spoke with Valerie a few times and to Rash; there were lots of things to arrange. We were going to cater in Shirley's kitchen for a final time. I would take with me smoked organic sea trout, Orkney cheeses and Orkney oysters.

On the Friday night I thought I would give Rash a ring. He answered, "Andrew!! Thank God you phoned. Your ears must have been burning." "What's up, Rash?" I enquired. "It's the ashes, we ain't got 'em. All the Turks are arriving, the Dutch are here, everybody is in London and I ain't got them BBBBbbbbbbldng ashes!"

"Don't panic — (Mutch)" was my advice. Rash spluttered "Val was meant to get them from Mortlake Crem. and didn't." "Why don't you get them, Rash?" was my response. "Because it's shut. The office is shut, the answer phone is on and it won't open until Monday when it will all be too late, and I'm in the proverbial THOU KENS WHAT." "Calm down young cousin," was my advice. I continued thus: "For in the face of adversity, oft can be drawn triumph from where it will be least expected". "Shut up" Rash retorted. (He was going into severe panic mode). "You've got the urn I made her, haven't you?" "NO!! That's at the blessed Crem' too." "Have any of the folk coming seen the funerary crock?" I enquired. "No, only Val, and she handed it over and no one can get it." "I'll phone Val then. Stay there and don't move, I'll ring right back."

Val answered, I could feel that cold sweat of hers when she heard my voice. "Is it true about Shirley's cinders?" I probed. "Yes, Andrew. It's all too horribly true." I suggested emailing. "I've done all that, it's no good. Rashid was meant to organise this bit, he said he'd do it later, there was plenty of time." "Poor Val" I soothed. "Look! I'll phone Rash back and develop a plan. I'll get back to you." The phone slipped from her clammy hand.

Rash answered in half a ring tone. "Andrew!! Anything??" "No joy." I informed him. I could hear tearing of tight frizzy hair down the telegraph pole. "Now Rashid!! Listen. Have you still got that big blue casserole that I made Shirley 30 years ago?" "Yes" he informed me "Good!" I replied. "Then this is what we do. I have got the oysters for the buffet. What I propose is that I open quite a few of them. Sigrid and I will enjoy them with the special shallot sauce I make. I shall then proceed to burn their shells on our open fire." Rash leaped in with: "What will Sigrid think?" So I told him "Oh! She'll be quite sporting about it, don't worry." "What next?" my cousin implored. "Keep cool, laddie" I advised. "This is the rest of the plan. I will bring the burnt crushed crustaceans in a poly bag. I shall also furnish us with some pure beeswax. We can tip the ashen shells into poor Shirl's cooking pot and seal the lid with the moulten wax. We can leave a few dusty remains on the lid, some of which will adhere to Nature's solidifying adhesive. This will lend a touch of homemade authenticity to the whole thing. And NOBODY WILL KNOW!"

"Andrew!!" Rash ejaculated, "I knew you'd come up with something. You've saved me. Phew!"

Sigrid and I enjoyed the Orkney Seafayre oysters and the glowing fire.

I phoned Val. I told her the plan; Val asked: "What do I do?" I directed: "Collude, collude" I noted her relief and consent.

Sigrid advised that I took my raincoat. I did.

I landed at Gatwick and was soon at Shirley's home.

Rashid greeted me. His girlfriend brought excellent things for the buffet too. We organised the drinks. But before all this I asked Rash who the undertakers were. "Don't know. Somewhere in Chiswick High Street I think." I Yellow Paged. There were three. I phoned Val. "Pling" went the phone when she answered it. "Who was the Undertaker, and what is their phone no.?" She related the vital digits to me. I hung up, then I entered them into the neat little keyboard on poor, late Shirley's handset. A recorded response emitted, advising me of a further sequence of Arabic numerals to punch in. I did as recommended. I reached a man in a van, he appealed for me to wait whilst he manoevered his transport into a lay-by.

I reported " My aunt has died" He said "I'm so sorry". I informed him that he probably wasn't sorry at all, as he had done the funeral, got paid and probably still had her ashes and the urn. He replied to me: "that is very likely, Sir". I thumbed up to Rash. I asked him his name. "Burnie" he replied. "Apt" I responded. "Well, Burnie. If you can root out Shirley's remnants and deliver them here by this evening, there's a Royal Bank of Scotland £20 note waiting for you." Burnie's urgent request was auntie's full name, address and interment No. I phoned Val, elicited the code and reported back to Burnie. He said "Thank Gaud for that! We don't want any mix ups with the ashes, do we?" "Not at this stage, no!" I answered. The hursuit driver arrived 97 minutes later and exchanged urn and contents for that fresh, new note. "Andrew" Rash said, "I don't know how you do it!" I answered, "Yes you do, you watched me, didn't you?"

Sunday morning arrived. Friends from all parts appeared. Of course they were sad, but we made it a lightsome occasion. It was pouring with rain and Shirley loved the rain (Pour Shirl). After the refreshments, wines and mineral waters and midday buffet, we wandered Thames ward. It was Shirley's dear wish to be hurled into that River. It was her Ganges. Rash knew a riverside pub with a pier. We all followed him. A procession of macs and brollies. Rash led with the tall urn aloft.

It caused quite a sensation when we all entered the riverside pub and Rash requested permission to fling his mum into the torrent from their waterfront, especially during their busiest lunchtime for weeks. The request wasn't denied, but Shirley's downpour had raised the water level well up the pub's Nile meter and we were all in great risk of being swept away, had we ventured to the spot Rashid desired.

Lo and behold, a little down river was a wee, ruinous jetty with a disused diesel pump for passing thirsty flotillas at its furthermost point. We ventured there. A squeeze past a part derelict workshop and along some sodden duckboards, the funeral procession slithered. We placed Shirley in her vase on top of the rusting pump. The varying folk with their faiths paid their last respects. I tilted her lid and sprinkled some burned oyster shell as a kind of marine dedication. The Olympic rowing team forced themselves upstream, completely unaware of our presence. As they passed, and in their wake Rashid hurled mater into the water. A splendid splash as she entered those swift depths. Her urn would revolve on the riverbed spilling her quenched cinders liberally. The lid will have parted from the pot as her soul escaped from her body.

Flowers were cast to float away on the grey river. What was exceptionally strange was that a Selkie bobbed its head above the Thames and looked straight at Rashid, then dived beneath. The last time Rashid had witnessed this was at Westness on Rousay whilst beach walking with his mum.

Cheers... Andrew

Rash with the ash

28 Blewits

*'Never before had we witnessed such a sight. Slowly,
carefully, we knelt amongst the fallen prickles of past seasons.
This shrine offered us its bounty, respectfully we gathered'*

The Kentish Autumn signals the wonderful colouring of the woodland foliage. This season is one of a nature's harvester's favourite times. Our family walks to the woods then, garnered us chestnuts, the last of the summer berries, hips and haws, fallen wood for the fire, and FUNGI.

I was the littlest of Madge's brood, not only did I often lag behind in my short, worn, black rubber wellies and baggy shorts, but being the smallest of the troop, I had to run to catch up, then hunt through the thickest of bushes for out of reach goodies. I thus learned the smells of the woods, that thick, leafy scent of the first fallen leaves, sometimes with a hint of frost. In these thickets lay nuts, which bigger ones couldn't get, these were for me to retrieve.

Those woodland forays were always an excitement. Mum (Madge) would always be on the earnest look out for our Patron Saint of Autumn... the BLEWIT. These special fungi hid amongst those foliate droppings of the season. They needed that frosty rhyme of evening to chill the leaves and begin their desiccation on woodland floor, ideal for blewit growth. That musty smell of oak, ash, chestnut and birch could be the clue to a Blewit stronghold.

The blewit, like the truffle, is a capricious wee "animal." You will find him or her under a bush one year, and never again!!! You will hunt all afternoon and see nought. Your paper carrier bag gets dampened, and the contents slip out of the corner. You have to back track and pick up the trail of chestnuts and stuff them into your woolly hat, then catch up with the rest of the Applebys disappearing into the woody gloom. Suddenly, the cry of "BLEWITS" blares out.

Then a hush, followed by the rustle of leaves being turned back in search. When I caught up the excitement was over. Maybe five or six of these scarce gems had been eased from their mouldering bed.

The top surface of this delicacy is smooth, like liver. It can be a musty blue or indeed brown with almost the hue of a kidney. It is the underside and stalk, which assure the identity of this wee creature. A violet blue is the colour of its gills and upper stem. It smells of woods and leaves and history. It has an ancient aroma, one of nature re-inventing itself in another being. When being tossed in a pan with a little bacon and served on toast with a fried egg, it enters into higher world of beings entirely... US.

The find spots of blewits were kept as firm family secrets, just in case they disobeyed their capricious nature and returned. It always left us hope for another year anyway.

A favourite blewit tale was when Madge, a friend Muriel and I were searching Well Woods for these elusives. I would have been at that annoying age of fourteen, but blewits always focussed the mind. We walked for hours, hoping and hunchbacked, stooped and peering in our quest. Ages went by...Nought!! At last we decided to go home with empty bags and saddened hearts. On our way back was a solitary holly tree with its branches weeping down to the ground. It created an impenetrable screen, like a wigwam, perhaps fifteen feet in circumference. I remembered my "tiny-hood" days and those worn booties. "Madge, Muriel!! Wait for me, I'm going to seek 'neath that holly canopy." They immediately idled on the spot, and chatted hopelessly of the lack of this and that and blewits in particular.

From within the innards of that holly tent, my eyes accustomed themselves to the dim. As my pupils dilated, the dark, dank scene unveiled itself. There, spread before me were BLEWITS. Then BLEWITS. Then MORE BLEWITS. I was wordless. It was like a blewit dream. Everywhere I peered blewits were waiting for me. It was one of those, almost holy moments when St. Blewit appeared.

Idling Muriel and Madge were about to slink off when I called out,

"Blewits" softly. They thought I was calling to the fungi in vain, for it to appear. (As we oft did) "No," I croaked, "I have fallen on a plethora" My failing voice added drama and conviction to my statement. M&M's approach was ginger. In half belief they craned their necks through the "Tee Pee's" entrance. I eased the foliate flap further aside. They entered and gazed on this marvel. Never before had we witnessed such a sight. Slowly, carefully, we knelt amongst the fallen prickles of past seasons. This shrine offered us its bounty, respectfully we gathered the larger, mature blewits. We were in the poly bag era now, and each of ours was empty, except, perhaps, for one of those useful little foldaway rain hats, which were so popular in the sixties. They tied up under your chin, you know, and they always smelt like the bottom of a raincoat pocket, the pleats adhering to themselves. They seemed to open reluctantly, the folds being stuck together with 'Residue'. I digress, back to the thrill of that scene in the Wilds of Kent. We filled our bags with this 'Manna'. There was still a carpet of fledgling blewits remaining to grow into full blewit-hood. We could return, just to see how they were getting on. In a few days we did, having been able to invent more recipes for them, such was our devotion to St. Blewit.

After moving to Orkney, there were only three things that I missed, bar- billiards, runner beans and, of course, BLEWITS. I searched Bisncarth Woods, eyed up Happy Valley and peeked under wee bushes and whins. Not a sniff of blewit – KNUFFINK – I accepted my loss.

Kind Caleb Walter, fer Nearhouse, gave me about five trailers of ancient rotted midden to level my garden with. This treasure heap sported a forest of dochans. (If only I'd have known about Dochan Spinach). Anyway, as this manure rotted, to me, unbeknown spoors were taking heed of their new environment. Autumn Equinox came and went, I did the Aviemore Trade Fair and returned. The dochans had been blasted away, and on my front patch, up Tramp Street, was a livery coloured mass. I couldn't believe the sight and I knew they couldn't possibly be blewits. I passed them by for two days, then, like Pooh Bear, I thought that it wouldn't hurt just to take a closer look. I couldn't believe it, blewits, blewits, blewits!!!! Like a second coming, there they were, blessing the sod of my yard. I picked, I plucked, I parted these angels from mid their midden. I phoned Madge. Breathlessly I told her, "Blewits in the gaaarrden!!"

How we reminisced, the holly B's never returned, she'd had two from up the lane and no more, a few from Well Woods and nine others, reached from beneath a fence on the edge of the Common. I tupperwared some of mine up for Madge and Muriel, post haste they were mailed off. They were received as myrrh would be. Those Grimeston blewits never returned either.

I am very relieved to say that over the years, I have found some

"Special Places" which Sigrid and I frequent. These happen to be on Orkney's high, windswept cliff tops. We have, therefore, discovered the whereabouts of the Field Blewit. They grow in vast fungal fairy rings. These rings, ever expanding, must be centuries, or millennia old, so large are they. Some rings "fall" off the cliffs and brave little and large blewits can be collected on the very edges, clinging to a grassy tuffet a hundred or two feet above the roaring sea. Erosion has sectioned them thus, and in some places you can even detect another part of the ring, separated by a gulf and time, arching but endlessly growing, on a nearby promontory.

We are fortunate indeed to have a little land attached to our house in France. This potager of ours is bound by the tiny river Ceur, and our farming neighbour delivers us great loads of manure there to grow our pumpkins on. After a couple of years of pumpkin bounty, Sigrid and I were delighted to find, after the frosts, a healthy picking of blewits. Our French friends were horrified when they heard we actually ate them. We were happy for them to remain suspicious and leave well alone. They are a greater rarity there than in the British Isles, and their secret lies with us still.

A favourite brunch we make from blewits is a soufflé omelette. So if you see Sigrid and me stooping suspiciously close to an Atlantic precipice of an early morning, you might realise what we are up to. But please, please, don't tell no-one, will you.

Thanks... Andrew.

*Son Nick carefully concealing
a blewitt under heel*

29 Rowan of Fursbreck

*'Perhaps he just wanted to keep the memory of Tressness as it was,
I don't know. We walked to the dunes. I looked back to the car,
and to my absolute horror, the tide had risen, not receded!'*

September's 'Now And Then Note' introduced a certain character, namely, James D Rowan. Jim, or Jimmy, deserves more than just a mention. He was an Orkney entity in his own right. His history is a little known, but an important one.

I first heard of him when I was about four years old, perhaps five. My father used to speak of his old Wartime comrade in the Orkneys. I learned that Rowan was the first official on the scene at the Brig O' Waith to record the first casualty of the Second World War on British soil. Yes, the poor unfortunate Orcadian, killed by a German plane, casting off its bombs whilst limping home. Rowan told me years later what a difficult trip it was. The road from Stromness, where he was based, was pitted with bomb holes. He went there on his motorbike avoiding these "Traps for the Unwary". He didn't speak of his distress at seeing the victim, that was just like him.

My Dad and Rowan had an interesting War in the Isles. They shot plenty of ducks in the Birsay area. The Sabiston family are the experts on this phase of the hostilities with Germany. The ducks turned out to be farm ducks in very fine condition. Peace reigned when the plucked birds were shared with their breeder.

Tressness on Sanday was probably their favourite haunt; here they had another base for the Army Intelligence. Jim got to know so many Sanday folk who remained friends with him for the rest of his life. The ones of them I knew most was the Meil family. Olly Meil became Jim's particular mate. On that promontory, now deserted, stood the grand farmhouse of Tressness. The access was by car or motorbike across the sands of the bay. A wonderful place to race a bike against a horse. The storms they experienced there were momentous. He described to me how it was like being on a ship at sea in that building when the tempests were at their height.

In those days Tressness was a thriving community. The farm, the servants and families. The horse mill was in regular use. There were kye, sheep and pigs, ducks (not target ducks) hens and geese. There was always home brew and a dram. This is where Rowan (he liked to be referred to as Rowan) learned his brewing, a dark, rich and strong brew, thick and silky. The seals were a constant company for a lone soul. Rowan liked his privacy and would share it sparingly.

After his War he tried life out of Orkney very briefly. A bank in Surrey (I think) called him. He soon returned. Life in Orkney appealed to him and he bought the farm of Fursbreck. 'Fursbreck', a Norse name, means 'Waterfall in the wild country', or something like that. There was a small watermill there, which served the toonship. There was probably a Viking mill of old there too. Rowan continued the ancient tradition.

James D. had a passion for hens. He documented everything about them. What they ate, when they were let out, how many eggs, when they hatched. He checked the rainfall, maximum and minimum temperatures, when there was a frost, when there was ice in the water but: - Everything.

His hens led him into milling their feed. He got more birds. He sold his extra hen food. He installed a small powered mill. He took on local labour. Peter Aim, Johnnie Gray and lots of folk whom I can't keep track of. The mill grew, sheds were erected, Jim expanded with grants from the HIDB. The egg marketing board assisted folk to GET THEM HENS IN and export eggs. The egg packing station on the Ayre was going full pelt. Hen houses were being constructed all over the isles. Chickens were "IT." Fursbreck Feeds filled their crops. Their gizzards churned as eggs emerged in a seemingly unstoppable stream.

James Rowan expanded further. A MILL IN STROMNESS. It later became Mill Stores, and is now the Co-Op. Jim bought a sports car, a little MG, she was called Efy. That car was his pride. Johnnie Gray kept

it up to scratch with his engineering talents. In fact Johnnie kept all the machinery of the Empire moving. He was allowed to keep his own time and not answer to anybody. He looked after all the working parts and cared for them like the "coos in a byre."

Everything burgeoned until that fateful night when the Government announced the winding up of the Egg

Marketing Board. The Big Lion roared, and the "Little Lion" was no more. The egg industry collapsed like an overcooked soufflé. Unemployed hens were scratching for a living, and so was JDR. Efy had to fly the nest. The canteen at Fursbreck began to loose its aroma of mince and tatties, cloutie dumpling and custard. Jim thought he might just be able to hang on. The men built the last hen hoose way up behind the byres. Rowan could make his own feed, maybe the business could survive by vending a dwindling resource in the local egg market. Yes! He could sell eggs, but not enough. The end was nigh. The "Parsons Nose" of Fate had its final twitch. Resigned to what had to come, he paid off all local debtors. Fursbreck Feeds was wound up. Rowan retired.

Jim maintained a few hens out of interest. His home was an open house for the youth of the day, and apparently always was. It was open house to me when I was in my teens. Even later, when I moved up to rent the "State of the Art" chicken hoose, he let me bide in the ben end until I was fit to flit into that glorious edifice.

Jim had two loons from a Glasgow Home to stay in the summers, Tommy and Paul. They mixed in well with the other members of the 'Fursbreck Youth Club'. Being from the city, they weren't too accustomed to country ways, but it was good for them. They were encouraged to do motor biking in the fields and on green roads. There were the odd incidents with airguns and the occasional minor punch up. "Ah! Ha! Hold it right there!" Rowan would bark, "take heed, lads. What's going on? Stop! Don't move a muscle!" All these commands, issued like a veritable machine gun, were instantly obeyed. A short interrogation ensued. The source of the trouble was rapidly divined, at which point due reprimands were metered out; a hushed peace then reigned. And, so, boys will be boys, they did settle in and settle down given patience and time. I used to cook for the 'Fursbreck Summer Camp' and associates on a Friday evening. Usually a huge spaghetti, Rowan made the ice cream and between us we fed them until bursting. They then went and flung darts whilst we washed up.

On my visits to Sanday, I found out how highly regarded Jim was. I sometimes asked him if he'd like to go back. "No! All in the past" he'd say. Well, it was a few years ago when I pressed him again. "Would you like to visit your old friend Olly?" He said that he would. I arranged the trip. My son Nick came with us and also Eri, a Japanese lady who was studying Orkney Folk Lore.

There was a breeze on the sea when we left Kirkwall for our day trip. We landed at Loth. Quite different from earlier days. We went to the bay of Tressness. I looked to the tide and determined that it was going out. What thoughts were going through Rowan's heid when we sped over those firm sands? Nick wanted to drive. "Later" I said, "much later." We were nearing the dunescape of the peninsular. I looked at the water's edge. Yes! tide going out I assured myself. Just as a precaution, I decided to park our Volvo hatchback on a little grassy tuffet. Rowan said that actually, he couldn't quite make the walk to the farm. He'd be glad to stay where he was... In the car.

Perhaps he just wanted to keep the memory of Tressness as it was, I don't know. We walked to the dunes. I looked back to the car, and to my absolute horror, the tide had risen, not receded! Rowan was almost surrounded by salty ripples. The two front tyres and one rear were being lapped by wind-teased water. I had visions of doing that real life emergency programme. Eri, Nick and I got to the car. Rowan was delightedly happy watching birds with his binoculars, oblivious to the danger. We hauled him out and got him into the shelter of those sandy hills. We lit a little fire, lent him our coats and watched as the water rose, each tyre submerging 'neath the brimming tide.

I could look no longer. I resigned to roam with Nick and Eri; at least Rowan wasn't drowning or floating away to sea. One hour and twenty-two minutes later we returned. Volvo was high and dry. Never did I reverse quicker from any parking lot. The beach-party goers got into the car when it was safe on the sands, I chauffeured them rapidly off to Olly's at Greens Pot. We had beer and whiskey. Olly, in his eighties, was bright as a button, but no quick on his pins. All drink was extremely to hand, some loaf and a little 'Fly Cemetery'.

Nick, Eri and I left the old pals to chat alone. We went to do some very safe sightseeing. An hour and 49 minutes later we returned. A little further chat and we left Olly to his memories. The old friends were happy to have had that time.

On the Varagen, Rowan thanked us for a good day and became unusually chatty. I rather think he would have liked to do a re-enactment on that Emergency Programme. I certainly wouldn't have. But it was a grand day oot.

Andrew.
P.S. Olly died that year, Rowan, two and a half years later.

30 Christmas Special

'They were scary. The ducks nibbling at my little black wellies made me jump nervously, their bills clacking at my ankles and toes.'

Fortunately or otherwise, I am blessed with very distinct and clear memories, and in particular, detailed ones from my early infancy. I was a two and a tiny bit year old toddler when I first became aware of Noël. I was taken to Dunn's Department Store in Bromley for a gratuitous visit to meet Santa in his 'Grotto'. The boy ahead of me burst into violent, salty tears and had a "teenies" tantrum on Papa Noël's knee. He then kicked the old man's tibia and ran off screaming.

Mum urged me forward to clamber up. I was careful not to knock Santa's shin during my ascent. It struck me as I arrived on Lap Land, that this bearded spectacle smoked the same kind of tobacco as my Dad... "Special Nosegay". The smell was so distinktive. Claus's nicotined digits seemed to confirm this, especially as a tiny scrap of translucent, white fag paper was stuck to his lower lip.

After a short conversation, during which I checked out the hairs in his ears, he handed me from his sack a charming little wooden skittle set with an endearing red wooden ball. I gratefully slid from his thigh to allow the quivering girl behind me to take her seat. I didn't watch.

The 119 bus took Mum and me nearly home. We sat on the top and up front of the double decker. It made me feel like I was Rupert Bear on one of his Nutwood adventures. We walked across Hayes Common picking up dead birch branches, filling up the spare Dunn's paper carrier bag which we had gleaned for that purpose. So now we had kindling for the next morning.

We arrived home as it was darkening. My kind brothers did their very best to disillusion me over Santa's authenticity. I told them that I would always, and forever, believe in him — Just like Rupert.

It was getting daily closer to 'Turkey Season'. Dad's fish round finished at about lunchtime, and after a swift visit to the New Inn he was ready to take me to Dave Davine's farm at Downe (Up to Downe – we all laughed). It seemed such a long drive to this distant village in our rusty green van. Dad was lending a hand in the plucking shed. I played in the field where all the suckings from the road drains in Orpington were dumped. Black soil, gritty with eroded tarmac. But, lo!! There I espied a shiny silver sixpence in that dark morass.

Everything seemed so big. The hens in the yard had their beaks at my eye level. They were scary. The ducks nibbling at my little black wellies made me jump nervously, their bills clacking at my ankles and toes. Thank heavens and Father Christmas that the turkeys were suspended pendulously in the long, cold corrugated iron shed as their plumage filled the atmosphere. A duck's beak or nine dangled in a draught, their bodies giving momentum as they swung from their tied feet.

Dad's payment was a brown ten bob note and a florin. Then a game of snooker on Dave's vast baise table, the balls struck my nose as they scored in the pockets. A bottle or four of Guinness was consumed during this action.

Darkness, cold and sleet greeted my face as we made for the van. I was sat on the leather seat as a Hessian sack got flung by my bare, ankle-booteied, chilly legs. Something from within scratched my calf as it sped past. Dad seemed so pleased with himself. We passed the roadside chalk quarry, where vampire bats and phantoms thrived. Then home.

We entered 101 G.G.R., or as we preferred to call it, 'Appleby Mansions'. Dad greeted Madge on the kitchen doorstep and handed her the sack proudly. "It's the feet!!" he proclaimed. "MADGE!! I'VE GOT ALL THE FEET!!" Malcolm and Stuart rushed to the kitchen to experience first hand this excitement. Mummy (Madge) only just managed to conceal her own sheer delight.

The sackful was tipped into our china sink for de-mudding. Brothers two grabbed a left and a right and made puppets from them by pulling turkeys' tendons. Those feet opened and closed as my "frères" composed their Turkish marching song, whilst they wondered if they could get on to 'All Your Own' with Hugh Wheldon.

A kettle of warm water was tipped onto the floating heels

so that it was more comfortable for Madge to scrub them. I helped and wetted a sleeve, which cooled my upper arm as Mum rolled it up for me. I stood on the kitchen stool and leaned over watching Mummykins brushing clarts o' dung from 'twixt their tootsies.

The first feet came out clean, but as their washing water dirtied and thickened, the rest needed rinsing. It was deteriorating gradually as worst foot came forward. Dad took over the tricky task of sloushing these unscaled 'délices' as he rinsed his tonsils with a little of the 'Irish Dark Fluid'. After immersing a few of these ex-turkeys' amputated members in clear water (slowly darkening, incidentally) the odd ingrown ring from the turkey's chick hood was systematically wrenched off, revealing ossified aluminium traces welded to their leggiments.

While enduring this lesson in pédi-cuisine, Pater enlightened Mater and me with regales of fowl footed tales as the laundered extremities dropped from his hand into their simmering black enamel crater.

Those feet revolved gently in eddies as steam floated spirally upwards contrasting with the dark walls of their stew pot. Scales curled slowly off to float away from their dead hosts, or, lets think about it 'Hostesses'. (WHAAAAAAa...aaAAa.)

Sink emptied, 'U' Bend blocked, feet simmered. Daddy said "Turkeys' feet ;- you can't beat 'em" He gurned on about China, Paris, Madrid, Prague – all capitols of – "Foot Cuisine". The word 'consommé' was banded, 'Bullion de Pied de poule' got a mention. Madge was extremely patient.

And did those feet in patient time, simmer on that gas flame?.. Well!! Yes! They did. Dad discovered Malcolm and Stuart's abandoned marionettes on the "Living Room" floor. He raised the lid of that cauldron so that they too could have their broiling baptism amongst their flock of lost soles. As this lid was lifted and depressed, the stentch filled our dwelling.

I was very glad that "Beddie Bies" time had come to my rescue. I felt relief as my dormitory portal was firmly sealed and two wee leaded windows were eased to encourage sufficient draught to clear that "Foot Odour". A flickering pattern of light decorated my ceiling, cast from the parrafin stove.

Late that night Madge would have diligently strained the pedimential broth. The bones, the scales, the talons and toe-nails which gathered into a sticky lump in our white and blue enamel colander, could have been ejected next morning on to the compost heap.

Christmas Morning in Gates Green Road dawned. At the foot of my bed was a Gollywog looking fixedly at me. A wee 'Bobby Sock' liberally stuffed with a tangerine and a selection of seven nuts. Stuart and Malcolm were opening their array of GIFT too.

We must have played for hours, for at midday, Daisy (Grandma) arrived. (How that time sped). From her florid left hand, a shilling for Stuart, a sixpence to Malcolm, a threepenny bit for me. What treasure!!.

Christmas Dinner... Billy Cotton Band Show (how I Hated that) "Wakey-wakey!"

'Educating Archie' was better, and 'Life with the Lyons' a relief – but enough of this jolly nostalgia. Back to the point, Andrew!

We all sat round the oaken table, leaves extended to the fullest. A cracker, a merry balloon (I lied about the balloon). Soup; hot, thin liquid, with bits of loaf crust drifting, was served into my bowl. "What's this??" I urged. "Turkey foot broth with ducks" came Father's answer. "Best thing for you" he added.

How I cried and cried and cried.

Yours, Aye. And a very merry Christmas from Sigrid and me.

Andrew.

Footnote... Since those days, and all my time in Orkney, I have vowed never to cook a dickie birdie's toe.

31 Letter from France

'Gourdon Market'

*'He purchased 12 sheep's' tongues, 1kg of cheeks
from same breed and 8 lovely lambs' kidneys that
we are very partial to for Sunday breakfast.'*

Most Saturdays we go to Market in Gourdon, a small town with beautiful limestone houses forming a circle round the old part of town, a steep ascent to where the castle once stood.

One used to arrive breathless when the market was held up there. Now it is on a big parking area by the post-office, more convenient for stallholders and the public. It starts at 8am and finishes at midday. There is an abundance of fruit and vegetables, pork butchers selling every imaginable item from that generous beast; some find the ears (smoked) a delicacy. Fish stalls compete at either end; we go to the one who shouts himself hoarse, often indulge in a dozen oysters or 1kg of mussels, seldom the expensive fish, such as Dover sole, cod, monkfish, skate and names I do not know in English. Sardines and mackerel will have to do us. No point in buying salmon or crab as we can indulge in that in Orkney. There are bread stalls, cheese stalls (very tempting), ladies with their fresh farm poultry and eggs. There we have our favourite lady whose hens have a talent for laying double yolkers. There is an old ladies mafia with their small vegetable stalls, very bio with produce from their garden plots. The best buy from one of these are bottles (any kind of reused such) of walnut oil. For visual delight there is the Moroccan stall with glistening olives in great variety, big chunks of candied fruit, delicious plump prunes and apricots, all sorts of shelled nuts and so much else to admire that one does not mind the queue. In summer further stalls set up with seasonal produce such as asparagus (oh such a delight), melons, peaches, pumpkins, strawberries etc. and the Basque with his wonderful cured sausages, fillet mignon (for sale at Fursbreck Pottery) and wild boar. There are flowers, pot plants and bedding plants to cheer a wintry heart. The budget gets overspent each time – the market puts you in a good and generous mood and the poor folk have been up since crack of dawn bringing all the stuff – hopefully to take less away and repeat the performance two to three times a week elsewhere. With a croissant or a spring roll in hand we cross the road to one of the cafés for a strong espresso or a hot chocolate when its cold and watch le monde go by.

In earlier days we equipped ourselves with large decorative baskets as is the custom, but soon our arms ached and Andrew took himself off to a garden centre, where he bought a very large wicker basket on wheels, more for garden or log use I am sure than manoeuvring round a busy market, bumping into ladies shins or tripping them up. I keep my distance and carry my own generous basket, from time to time dropping the heavier items into his. Once Andrew went to market with two buckets when we had visitors from Scotland. I walked on the other pavement not wishing to know him. Our friends took pity on me and bought me a genteel basket.

The capital of Lot (our French region) is Cahors, an old Roman town, pleasantly situated by the river of same name. Like most towns it has its market day, taking place in the large square by the Cathedral. The Queen of Denmark goes shopping there with her very own basket during the month of August when she and her French husband Prince Henri are in residence at Château Caix. However, there is a covered market where you can shop every day for a great variety of beautifully displayed goods. Everything is of the best quality, the vegetables, fruit, butcher meat, oysters and fish. We note the price of smoked salmon – more expensive than ours and not bio. Fine wines and cheeses, beautiful and unusual flowers, again such a delight for sore eyes.

Yesterday we were in Cahors, where we usually treat ourselves to lunch, but we gave it a miss, maybe for financial reasons. Anyway it was haircut day for Andrew (not having had one since last time in

Cahors in October). While I stayed on and got turned into a strawberry blond, he ventured off on a couple of missions, one being a visit to the covered market. He purchased 12 sheep's' tongues, 1kg of cheeks from same breed and 8 lovely lambs' kidneys, that we are very partial to, for Sunday breakfast. The butcher was stunned: a BRIT buying such unusual cuts of meat and in such quantity. We had the

Cheeks (one third of them) last night, very nicely cooked by Andrew, I must admit, with shallots, cèpes and towards the end of the cooking some sliced endives (called chicory in English) steamed on top. A little wine and crème fraiche made up the sauce. I had to compliment him, but then he often does that to me.

He came to pick me up from the hairdresser and admired my changed appearance whilst I picked off some crumbs round his mouth. An onion tart he confessed – a very small one – tiny really!

Sigrid

Going to the market with friends

32 Letter from France

'Duck soup and more duck'

*'It seduces the tongue with its very
subtle texture and flavour.'*

At this time of year, late January through February, it is the duck season; not the shooting season, but the sorting out of the fattened fowl. I will not go into the details of force-feeding ducks and geese as the farmers practise in the region of Perigord, which the Lot belongs to.

Fewer now sit down to this enjoyable task, spending a social morning or a whole day, depending on the amount of ducks. People buy the cooked results in tins or in glass with lovely labels, and the leftover carcasses are sold for soup for a modest sum. What good value they are with strips of meat on the breastbone (useful for a stir-fry), fat for melting down (good for sauté potatoes) after which some crispy bits of skin remain to be guiltily enjoyed.

We had friends who observed this annual custom and they invited us to come assist and taste. They were Elian and Josette – now departed. He, sadly no longer breathes and she opted for an old people's home.

As I mentioned before ducks and geese are generally raised to enlarge their livers for the making of 'foie gras'. Home made foie gras is the absolute height of culinary enjoyment for the French. I refuse to make it, but I will gladly volunteer to eat it. It is like nothing else, not like liver paté (you must never refer to it by that name) – it seduces the tongue with its very subtle texture and flavour.

Back to Elian and Josette in their kitchen. The ducks were cut up on the table – the breasts were for freezing down, later to be cooked like steaks – the legs and wings were for confit. This is a very old way of preserving meat in general.

The pieces of duck are rubbed with coarse salt and put in a crock, sprinkled with pepper and more salt, thyme and bay leaves. Left covered for 6 to 12 hours whilst being turned now and then. When ready to cook, excess salt is removed and the pieces are transferred to a large casserole, skin down and cooked in the oven until the fat runs and the skin browns. A further cooking in fat for two hours until the meat is tender, after which the pieces of duck are packed into a large pot with either duck or goose fat. Then sealed with a cloth and paper. Kept cool the meat will keep for months.

At Elian's and Josette's all the leftover bits were cooked on the stove, they are called 'fritons', very naughty tasty bits of meat with crisp fat that we popped into our mouths. TIME FOR APÉRITIFS.

Sigrid

33 Letter from France

'About Elian'

'Sometimes we would find Elian sitting panting against a tree with his puffer in hand. We worried about him – rightly so.'

Our friend Elian, who I mentioned in my last letter, came to live in the Lot when he retired early from travelling all over the world as a marine engineer. He had worked in far-flung places such as Siberia, Madagascar, Aberdeen, Singapore, Peru, Nigeria and the US, which he liked the least. Best of all he liked Africa and it was in Senegal that his too large heart came to rest.

I say too large, because in fact it was, due to too much weightlifting in his younger days. So – he got heart trouble later on – in the other sense too, as he had sweethearts in many places and a child or three, besides his two French children.

He knew all about electrics and plumbing and was only too happy to solve our "domestic" problems. Once the job was done, we had long chats over coffee or apéritif. He had many stories to tell as well as a liking for philosophising about LIFE as he thought himself very wise. Not an intellect though, so he found refuge in DIY – 'bricolage', as is often the case with men when they retire. It gets them away from the wife; the workshop becomes the centre of their activities or sometimes just an excuse for being on their own. Most of us have this craving, I think.

Due to his heart condition, we helped him too – in his wood on a steep slope, we pushed a wheelbarrow loaded with chainsaw, handsaw and can of petrol uphill. We had a merry and exhausting time collecting the sawn off lengths in the barrow, taking it to the edge, where we flung them, sometimes triumphantly right down to a meadow, where we later gathered the logs and wheeled them to his old mill house – later to be shared between us. Sometimes we would find Elian sitting panting against a tree with his puffer in hand. We worried about him – rightly so.

Giving up was not his style. I recall his *last job* with us shifting a light fitting over our kitchen table which involved drilling and screwing into a very hard oak beam. I held him by his legs, as if that would help. I felt such guilt listening to his breathlessness and groans. This was just before he was going on holiday to Senegal with Josette. They came round to say "Goodbye", his arms weighed down with two plastic bags containing some rabbits for our freezer. He looked desperately thin and exhausted. Only he and his doctor knew that he had cancer. Elian had put all his papers in order in his workshop beforehand. He knew it was 'á dieu' not 'au revoir.'

We miss him!

Sigrid

Elian
Courtesy of Anne Christie

34 Letter from France
'Our neighbour'

*'He has a pedal organ, which he plays from time to time,
and which accompanies his singing; a very fine voice indeed'*

Our immediate neighbour is le Curé, the local pastor, who has lived in that unchanged house next-door most of his life. All we know about his past is that he went to Sorbonne University in Paris to study Music and Literature; a very rare incident for a son of a 'peasant' in deep rural France. Later he taught these subjects in a small town called Montcuq, where two of my grandchildren have been and two will later on go to College.

Being an exceptionally shy person teaching youngsters must have been quite an ordeal for him, so when his parents got old and frail, he decided to change 'career', and attended Seminar to become a priest. He returned to his parental home and took over the parish from a well-liked and outgoing Curé who shared his life with his parishioners. He had paid them visits, played cards with them and performed his pastoral duties as one might expect. Our Curé does none of this, simply because he cannot bring himself to be outgoing. Some people find this hard to accept, but as we are not churchgoers, we are able to forgive his almost unchristian ways. Instead we observe his simple lifestyle, so set in the frugal past, his knowledge of nature, all the names of plants in Latin, whether certain fungi are edible or not, insects, birds – just ask him and he will give you the answer.

He has various plots of land, which he tends in a very basic manner; his tools are all pretty ancient, but efficient and sufficient to him. His expenditure is also very minimal. You could call him a miser, but I doubt he earns much from his Sunday Masses, Funerals, occasional Christenings and

Weddings. His supplementary income has been selling the much-valued truffles that he has managed to find on his land.

The annual truffle markets take place in January through to March, where high bidding is the norm. This is the only place they are sold and bought, prices reaching over 300 Euro per kilo. Not an item you keep in your larder, except concealed in a tin of special paté. He once gave us a truffle; I sliced it thinly – bits at the time and soaked it with beaten eggs for an omelette. To me an overrated fungus; give me a morelle (also expensive) or simply other kinds of fungi and one is less nervous about ruining the result.

The Curé has a television; that is the height of modern acquisition as far as he is concerned; our TV set is for videos only. He has a pedal organ, which he plays from time to time, and which accompanies his singing; a very fine voice indeed, which I guess is the most significant contribution to his church services.

He hates most machines, not just for the noise they make, but because they do a job that he thinks should be made by hand. Much of his time is taken up by sawing wood. He once tackled a huge old dead oak tree by the road – such hard work, but he persevered until the local council decided to do the job for him. As the tree was on his land, he was provided with a good amount of firewood, which he keeps as 'reserve' in a barn.

One of the pleasures we have in common is FIRE! Bonfires, burning leaves, grass, whole meadows in fact. We have a meadow too, by the burn, and every other year we burn it, equipped with shovels to put out too fast advancing flames. Previous times le Curé came down, carrying his own shovel to help keep the fire in check. This year he did not appear and the fire got out of hand – so much so that I ran home to phone the fire brigade. Brave Andrew got the fire under control, missing an eyebrow or two plus a nasty burn on his hand. The fire brigade arrived eventually – though I had called off the emergency – and they had a chat with our neighbour as Andrew had fallen asleep, exhausted by his efforts and I had taken the grandchildren safely off to a skateboard park – not without its dangers either.

The meadow has remained black due to the very cold spell, but now as I write Spring has arrived with all its annual wonders. Will we see all the wild flowers, cowslips, violets, celandines, and the may blossom and more before we leave?

Sigrid

35 Letter from France

'Bliss'

'I would not trespass on his patch, so I went elsewhere and found a modest amount, enough for that "famous" breakfast of Andrew's.'

Bliss is the word that comes into my mind at irregular intervals. This late spring and early summer seems the loveliest that I remember. Apart from a cold start, everywhere in Europe was chilly; gradually the days became silky warm. Our roses burst into bloom as the fragrance from the Philadelphia and privet bushes lingered in the nostrils. The meadows are still full of mauve, pink, orange and yellow, just as a Monet palette.

Sufficient rain tumbled down to raise the level of the "burn", just as it freshened our garden. The grass needed cutting yet again, but luckily I can still push the old loyal mower. The Farmers have cut the hay, but some meadows are left in all their loveliness to the joy of butterflies and bees – and me.

I like the evenings becoming dark gradually, from ten o'clock and after, as I am able to sit outside stargazing. I watch the night planes, seemingly as high up as the stars. I imagine the people suspended in the universe whilst being served drinks, and at the same time watching "B." movies. The nightingales begin their amazing trills in the hedgerows, the bell frogs join in with the crickets, and if I am lucky I can discern the almost silent flap of the owl's wings heading for our pigeon tower.

Another form of Bliss is a pretend siesta in my newly acquired reclining garden chair; this leaves you in a perfect position to slumber and read. I have been devouring books, serious and amusing for hours on end without any sense of guilt at all.

To my credit I did entertain an Old Danish friend from

pre-school days, and also through life. She stayed for two weeks with me. It was Bliss too, driving with her through pretty, to stunning scenery with Medieval castles dotted about, the Dordogne River weaving its way through the landscape.

Our furthest visit was to the Bordeaux region where we were invited for a day and a night to stay in an architecturally very harmonious wine chateau. The owner is Danish and exports his Premiéres Côtes de Bordeaux to the Scandinavian counties. I bought two cases, which I shall lay down until our return in October.

Our neighbour, the Curé, gave me some chanterelles the other day. He has the eye and nose for finding these elusive fungi. I would not trespass on his patch, so I went elsewhere and found a modest amount, enough for that 'famous' breakfast of Andrew's .

Perhaps we will be 'blissed' with field mushrooms in Orkney this summer. Soon no more chilled Rosé under the parasol, no feet in the air, but firmly on the floor at Fursbreck Pottery – for a while anyway.

Yours truly ... Sigrid.

PS. the first of the very old white lilies has opened, facing the morning sun, whilst I'm having that special breakfast in the garden ... Bliss.

36 Letter from Denmark

'An August visit'

'If only Orkney would adopt a more colourful attitude to conservation, we might not suffer from too much greyness.'

My favourite time of day in France is breakfast in the garden; in Denmark it is siesta under the old pear tree in my friend Lis's garden, combined with reading and afternoon tea. A morning or early evening dip in the sea is high on the list of favourite doings too.

We were busy as well. When Andrew was here the first week, we took part in a great nephew's christening. He was two years old on that day. Blond and blue eyed, he walked dressed in a sailor suit up the isle with his parents. Times have changed!

My half cousin celebrated his 80' birthday, a very elegant lunch in a renowned hotel called Marienlyst right by the sea and overlooking Kronborg (Hamlet's) Castle. We drank nothing but champagne and I did not complain.

Andrew went for early morning walks in a nearby wood – the rest of us still asleep in our beds. He has a special friend in the village with whom he talks ancient flint (Jørgen has a formidable collection) and drinks beer.

I joined old school mates, twelve of us, at the Karen Blixen Museum, which was the childhood home of the author and where  she returned to live and write her stories after her stay in Kenya. It is a beautiful house with a park, the interiors reflecting a bygone era that some of us regret the loss of. The commercial side of the place is tastefully done, like most such things in Denmark and we enjoyed a light lunch followed by coffee or tea at the nearby home of the Danish friend who visited me in France early summer. She had made a great effort laying two tables with all her best china and silver, cakes in abundance and shortbread from Harray Stores.

Before washing up the precious stuff, we borrowed a bike for me and Bente took me for a two-hour ride, so I was saddle sore for two days. Next day into Copenhagen to see the magnificently restored Christian VII' Palace, part of the royal Amalienborg. Built as 'town houses' for the nobility, forming a circle round a spacious octagonal square with a bronze statue of King Frederik V in the middle. This is where the Queen resides part of the year, guarded by the famous royal guardsmen in their bearskin hats – they were obviously suffering in the heat (27°c) that day.

These days one is very security conscious, but I was still surprised to hear the guards shout across the square. Some tourists with rucksacks were sitting against a wall. They could not understand the message 'get away from the walls' in Danish, so I did my bit as interpreter.

Later we took a boat trip round the harbour and the canals. We got a close-up view of the new Opera house with water on 3 sides of it, not quite Sydney, but still impressive; the Royal Yacht and a rear view of the Little Mermaid. I am not surprised tourists take to Copenhagen in a big way.

The country is enjoying an economic boom with very low interest rates, so people are borrowing lots of money and doing up their houses. I noticed many newly thatched buildings, often, old converted farmhouses painted in the characteristic ochre yellow or red. If only Orkney would adopt a more colourful attitude to conservation, we might not suffer from too much greyness. The farms are mostly beautiful and without the mess round them that we see here, but maybe the Orcadian farmers would have a word or two about the Danish farming practises- I am hardly qualified to judge.

I think it is up to Andrew to describe the lunch we had in Copenhagen at the Canal Café where we lunched together 13 years ago. Everything was unchanged, except the prices I suppose, but it was certainly good value- and very filling. We shall return again.

Sigrid

37 Letter from Denmark

'A Danish lunch'

'Another was ordered. I couldn't believe my eyes – they seemed quite sober and orderly, but I know what a few glasses of snaps do to me!'

I mentioned in my earlier Letter From Denmark that Andrew would be writing about the lunch we had in The Canal Café in that lovely old part of Copenhagen. He has asked to be excused, so I will try and recall the experience.

The café is situated conveniently close to the Danish Parliament where some less health-concsious members like to lunch. You step down to a former cellar, and the further you venture in, the smaller the rooms; one table sits on its own right under the stone stair that once led to the cellar. The atmosphere could be claustrophobic, but it is so convivial that you forget about possible fire hazzards. The nicotine-stained walls are covered with old marine pictures and relevant souvenirs.

The menu list of open sandwiches is long and tantalising; they were a total delight to hungry eyes and set our gastric juices going. Should I spoil it by saying that they probably also had an adverse effect on our inner organs, such as liver, arteries and intestines? No!

It wasn't so much what WE ATE (Two each) but what the four people at the table next to us consumed. It was their annual visit – they took all afternoon about it – well, they would have to. When we

arrived and placed our modest order, they were tucking into their first platter, a huge communal salver with a plethora of various kinds of marinated herring, with their garnish of raw red onion, capers and tomatoes. The herring was washed down with generous measures of snaps (Aquavit) as tradition has it. I don't think they quite cleared the dish, but the level in the snaps bottle had lowered considerably.

Next, another fish platter, which I would have liked to have got a closer view of, and a taste or two. There were warm fillets of breaded plaice, shrimps, crayfish, caviar, smoked salmon and perhaps other items that only politeness prevented me from seeing. Salad garnish with great helpings of home made mayonnaise. This required more snaps to go down the gullet – a few token slices of bread (Rye and Sour Dough) slipped under some mountains of shrimps, or whatever, through the meal.

By the time the third salver arrived their snaps bottle was empty!! Another was ordered. I couldn't believe my eyes – they seemed quite sober and orderly, but I know what a few glasses of snaps do to me!

This was the meat course. There was dinner for twelve, I reckoned. I glimpsed meat balls (Danish Frikadeller,) roast pork loin with crackling, salted silverside, rolled pork breast, homemade liver paté with aspic jelly and what else? I hope no more. Pickled beetroot and gherkins to cope with the fat. Yet another toast, draining their glasses, then more beer as well.

By this time Andrew and I had finished our two each open sandwiches, which were so good and filling that we decided one each would have sufficed, or perhaps just sharing three. The lovely beer served in large tankards certainly helped the digestion and general amiability. The crunching sound of crispy pork made Andrew sigh with envy, but it was time for coffee for us – the others still had the cheese tray to look forward to – or not as the case might be. We wished them 'Bonne Continuation' as the waitresses say in France, and then strolled off to The National Museum.

I couldn't help wondering how the two couples would be feeling that evening. We had to resort to lots of mineral water, what about them? I hope they are still alive and ready to celebrate next year – in a Spa perhaps.

'Velbekomme' Sigrid

38 Letter from France

'Snails'

'I must say, served up in a very garlicky, herby butter sauce with fresh pasta, it was a dish well worth remembering. Worth all that trouble I am not too sure about, but somebody else can do it next time.'

As whelks are sometimes named 'sea snails' according to Andrew, perhaps we can refer to these snails as land whelks. The English, as we know, teasingly call the French 'Frogs' because they consume frogs' legs, which actually are a delicacy. Personally I do not go out of my way to eat them, as I am fond of the little jumpy creatures in their natural habitat.

Snails are another matter entirely. I have often chosen them for a starter in a restaurant, prepared for you and served with that special gripping utensil, so you can drain the shell of its delicious garlic and parsley butter sauce, whilst trying to avoid this running down your chin or worse down your best clothes, before extracting the snail and chewing its flavoursome rubbery body.

Now!! The other day my son James, who flits between France and Scotland, arrived for a brief visit from La Charente Maritime, famous for its oyster and mussel beds, bringing a couple of very welcome megrim, some scallops and as a special treat for Andrew, a netted bag of snails, named 'petites gris', different from the larger white Burgundy escargots. My delight was more modest with regard to the snails as, although they were a present for Andrew, the task fell on

me with regard to the preparation. Out came the book on Regional French Cooking and I understood why nobody that I know of would want to do what I was about to do.

I must first say that these snails had already been purged, i.e. starved for a week in a ventilated box, sprinkled with water to keep them moist. Then, suddenly they are fattened on flour, which cleans them out. These snails have been grown commercially in so-called snail parks (an ancient practice) and usually the rest is done commercially too, like the cooking, de-shelling etc.

So what I did first was to rinse and soak them, after which pleasant treatment they started to emerge, tentacles poised from their shells. Then came the cruel bit: I put them in a large pan with a cupful of coarse salt and shook them vigorously, which drove out their sticky juices – and killed them, I think. After a final rinse I simmered them for two hours in water, flavoured with herbs, peppercorns, salt and some white wine. When cooked and drained I extracted them from their shells and removed the end bit, which was their stomach. Not an exercise I long to repeat. However, I must say, served up in a very garlicky, herby butter sauce with fresh pasta, it was a dish well worth remembering. Worth all that trouble I am not too sure about, but somebody else can do it next time.

It reminds me, that at home in Stromness there lingers a tin of snails – somehow the occasion has never presented itself to serve them up – now I know what to do – I only have to invite somebody special to share them with us. Who will it be?

Sigrid

39 Letter from France

'Tomato soup'

'We think upon this with horror, but to think that this still happens, all be it illegally, fills one with even more shame.'

Some weeks ago we visited my daughter-in-law, Jude, and grandchild Freya, who live temporarily near La Rochelle on the Atlantic coast of France. There, Freya attends a school attached to a music conservatory. She became bi-lingual within one year and has adapted to the rigorous French school system. Instead of moaning about hard work and long days, often ten hours, she accepted the challenge.

Anyway, on arriving we were served a delicious fresh tomato soup. Quite a surprise, as tomatoes were definitely not in season. In fact, they are often very tasteless and should not be grown in the winter, taking far too much water from the Spanish farmers where they are grown by Dutch villains. This is another, and bigger, subject for a proper journalist to explore. Jude's secret was that she roasted the tomatoes in her oven first and then blended them adding a bit of stock.

The other day, I bought a net-bag of those scornful tomatoes and decided to have a go at 'Jude's Soup'. I put the tomatoes in a handy little baking tray with some olive oil and herbs from our garden. After about half an hour, they came out crinkly and intact. I then blended

them with some chicken stock (cube would do) and a little cream, adding seasoning, including a slash from the chilli sauce bottle, freshly grated ginger, a cube of brown sugar, and a dash of balsamic vinegar. We enjoyed it in the garden for lunch (on an early April day) sheltered by our house from the north winds. The soup was served with little cheese scones and fresh goat cheeses.

La Rochelle is famous for its oyster, scallop and mussel beds. Huge fish markets made our eyes boggle with their sheer variety and abundance. The town used to be famous for its port, where thousands of slaves from Africa were sold and deported to America. There is a museum called La Nouvelle Monde dedicated to the history of the slave trade and other French exploits in Canada. We think upon this with horror, but to think that this still happens, all be it illegally, fills one with even more shame.

La Rochelle and its offshore islands are now fashionable summer resorts, especially for the Parisians. We are less fashionable in the Lot, but it's definitely a very pretty region. Many farmers still hang on to their mixed agriculture, growing a variety of fodder, walnut trees for nuts and oil of course, vegetables and fruit. They keep ducks and hens, handsome cattle graze the lush fields, whilst others are occupied by sheep and goats. Beekeeping is another traditional pursuit, and the honey they produce is delicious indeed; All very wonderful products, which end up in the local butcher shops and markets. The farmers also own woodlands where the trees provide firewood and various kinds of mushrooms including the truffle. Some of these farmers are hunters at the weekend during the season, wearing camouflage and bright red hats! Their targets are wild boar and deer and the occasional hare. These are for their own and friends' consumption only, definitely not allowed for sale!

Every February their is a special 'Hunters' Repast' in the village halls with so much to eat and drink that it makes you wonder how anyone can manage it. We did it once with our potter friend Jean-Pierre: We had apéritif, then bean soup, followed by salad with cured sanglier, after that, roast venison with flageolet and garlic. The roasted pig as well, was served with sautéed potatoes and wild herbs. The cheeses came next with new supplies of vin rouge. Fruit tarts for dessert followed not much later... then coffee... after a generous libation of 'Eau de Vie' in this case, vieux prunes.

We don't think we could cope with that experience again.

Sigrid

40 Coping with cancer

'F.A.R.T.S.'

Ionce referred to the above condition (though not by it's current title) in my 'Now And Then Note' entitled, 'It's a Parsley Nuisance'; that was before I had Monty, my laptop, and his wonderful 'spell check'.

The fact is that although parsley is good for clearing a 'short stay' affliction, it may not always manage a semi to long term one. Sigrid advised another visit to Dr Hazlehurts Den for a parlaiance. On her second appeal, I took her advice and arranged a visit to the afore–mentioned practitioner.

My dialling digit went into connection mode and I was assured of an appointment the very next morning. I turned up promptly to face that barbed, Hippocratic Oather. I readily reported to him the return of my Frequently-Acute-Rectal-Turbulence-Syndrome, to which he offered, if not empathy, genuine and fulsome sympathy.

I was asked pertinent questions concerning the frequency of occurrence. Whether or not I experienced any internal pain? (No) Had I lost my appetite? (No) Had I lost any weight? (No) What had I thought it was due to? (Change of diet).

The good doctor asked me to 'Assume the Position' as he glanced firmly couch-wards. I did, I became for a short while a couch banana whilst his gentle prodding and probing tried to elicit pain or lumps and bumps. Neither was forthcoming. A blood test followed, then the now familiar request for a 'sample'. I was handed again a dinky little screw topped, clear plastic tube with a sportily modelled, blue, polytex, diminutive shovel, conveniently attached to the lid.

My thoughtful physician explained that there was no real need to pack it full to the gun wails. The analysts only required 'a Drop! They weren't growing roses!' I nodded assent and reversed from his chambers, phial in sweaty paw.

I returned post-haste with sampler's capsule enclosed within a used manila envelope. This passed from my left hand to his right as he sauntered by in the waiting vestibule of the new Dounby Healthcare Centre. I was to await his call as to the result the next day or so. Patiently I potted as he doctored.

As sure as it rains in Indianapolis, the good doctor called and sent for me. It seemed that there was a dysfunction somewhere and Dr Bob recommended a routine ultra sound examination. This was fixed up quite rapidly, as Sigrid and I were due to follow the swallows to sunnier climes. A few days later I was summoned to Balfour. I thought this extremely efficient.

When I arrived for the look-see in my abdomen at my afternoon appointment, I read with interest the further notes on 'Preparing for an Ultrasound Examination'. They informed me to fast for 12 hours before. Whaaaa! I hadn't read that bit. I thought quickly. What had I had … nothing! No breakfast, no elevenses. Ah! But Sigrid had made our pottery lunch. Phew! I had only had a couple of forks full of coleslaw.

I admitted this to the nice ultrasound lady. Then ensued a fascinating conversation on coleslaw.

I was told that the pictures would be e–mailed to Aberdeen and I would hear soon from the specialist, via Dr. Hazlehurt's.

I went straight away to a meeting of the Arts Forum. It was a very positive gathering and most rewarding to be at.

When I got back to the pottery, Sigrid told me with a concerned expression, that Dr H had rung me. He needed to see me for a discussion. It was too late to visit him that day, so I rang his number and Sheila answered. I was inked in for a 12.30 appointment the next day. I asked Sigrid to come with me.

41 Coping with cancer

'Black Friday'

This is the difficult part to start telling, but I have to begin. Sigrid and I were duly waiting in the Dounby Health Centre's vestibule. As is my wont, I did a tour of the pot plants. The central heating does affect these 'Captives of the Planters'. If they could shout "Water! Water!" they would. Instead I had to write them a little prescription saying "H<z6.000>2<z$>O. In liberal doses" This usually has the desired effect.

The good practitioner, Dr R Hazelrust, ushered us in. After asking after his health and spirits, I enquired after mine. This must always be a bad time for doctors. My ultra sound results had been examined. Sigrid and I could see that the news was not agreeable. This was a point when we could also see the real humanity and compassion of my GP. He had to explain that there were areas on my liver, which were almost certainly cancerous, and inoperable.

This was of course, a complete shock to us. We had to take in the news. We held hands. We tried to take stock. But you just can't in those brief moments when you hear something as devastating as that. We asked Robert: "What is going to happen now?"

"More tests I'm afraid," was 'Black Friday' Bobby's reply. He added that they weren't yet absolutely positive whether it was cancer, but they had to go down that road of examination. He was going to arrange for an appointment at the Balfour for some internal lookings about. 'Up the way, and down the way.' (These weren't his exact words, but the drift was got.)

This shock was the biggest Sigrid and I have ever had to bear together.

We sat, trying to take Dr H's words in. I was shaking, Sigrid, pale. Could this possibly be true. She asked me if, having found this out, did I want to present the Request Programme on Radio Orkney that night? It was my shift. She was worried for me. I said: "When you hear news like this, you have to face it. You have to go on. It is not going to go away and if you hide from it, you succumb. I'm not going to!"

Dr Hazelhruts said to us that it was the positive attitude which should beat this thing ...

He explained to us that I would have to have a chest X ray. This was to establish if I had a lung cancer as well, or even a bowel or stomach cancer. This news was worrying. I thought of all the chest pains I had ever had. I wondered if my stopping smoking nearly 14 years before had been just too late. He had to be straight with us. It was hard, but life is like that. It was hard for my doctor too.

Our meeting came to a conclusion, and it was time to take our leave. The spider plants looked refreshed, as did the begonia, their 'prescriptions' having been administered. We drove back some of the way and parked by the loch just past the Merkister. It is a beautiful spot, and one where you can feel the nature of Orkney and take things in. Water, white swans, clouds, sky and hills. This is where we sat for a good while.

Angus walked past us with his dog. It was a time for Sigrid and me to be alone together before we had to share this with our friends and family. Our plans for the immediate future were 'on hold'. We could only plan for 'now' and even then, nothing was really up to us. My saying of 'Man plans, and God laughs' seemed apt, though I didn't think that God was feeling the least bit jovial over this. Angus turned with his dog and walked towards us. We drove away and waved. It was not a moment to be asked: "How are you?"

It so happened that I was giving tuition to a Potter from Glen Shee. When we returned to the pottery, she asked us how we had got on. Diana was our first friend that we had to tell. Of course she was shocked and sorry at the news. She suggested that she waived her tuition. We told her "No," we would rather have folk around us. She understood our plight perfectly. We found out then that she too had had to bear this herself, when she was told she had cancer some years before. She got over it; she had a harrowing time, but all is now well.

We however, were still assured, to a certain extent that this was not yet certain, and we clung to that hope, even though we had to prepare for the worst.

I am not the sort of person to give up and accept a fate which can be avoided. Talking with Diana helped us with this. She told us also, that even though we would go through depths of despair, as she did, there were the positive points too. Those positives are the things to hold on to. Grab them and keep them. When you hear this, you don't feel quite so alone. You realise that you are not the only one. Cancer can kill, but you can also live with it.

Diana and her amour, Bob, were to have dinner with us at home that night. We elected to give that one a rest. I did, though, do the 'Radio Orkney Request Programme'. This had a few awkward moments. The worst was when John Fergusson mislaid all the music. There was a golden wedding request, when I thought of the chances of longevity, briefly. Children's choices with, I am afraid, 'The Crazy Frog' and one thinks: "Have I got time for this?"

On the whole, though, it was a very positive experience. It taught me that commitments were there, and if you shirk them, then the quality of your life is diminished, and so, perhaps, of those around you.

I drove back past the silvery Bay of Firth, moonlight reflecting from the waters, and darkening shadows forming the Evie hills. This day was coming to a close, we have plenty more days to come, and each one must be of worth. Each day should be something special and one to be looked forward to. I began to think of the future.

I had not felt unwell, I felt fitter than I had for years, and life was good. The only thing that marred it was the bad news we had received that afternoon. In any case, doctors can be wrong!

When I got home, Sigrid had made a light supper. Diana and Bob's dinner was 'resting'. I suppose we weren't too hungry. I had a glass of wine, but had not the thirst for it. At these times you really feel what you mean to each other.

How do we tell our family? When? How do we let our friends know? Do we cancel any plans? These were all questions we talked about, and a lot more too. We knew there would be times for crying, and it is better to do just that. Sometimes to cry together and other times apart. We should face each difficulty and hurdle as it came. You have to be fit to leap hurdles, so we needed to keep sight of that.

This was our first cancer day, with a sleepless night ahead. I resolved not to take a pill, let's be aware on this night if that had to be. Then, later, we could take stock.

42 Coping with cancer

'Shayla steps in'

We did spend a night awake. The occasional drift of sleep. We had comfort in each other, but the early hours of the morning are often the lowest. Midnight tea sometimes helps. We talked the more at times; then lay quiet. My pillow was amuck with sweat. We were blessed with a sleep drift from about four until six thirty. Radio Four had soothed us all night, the volume low.

Life had to continue. I can't remember what we had for breakfast, though it will not have been one of our special ones. In 'Yesterday's' discussion with my facially hirsute physician, Dr Hazlehurst, our lives had been changed forever. This was a Saturday and the Pottery had to open.

It is strange how somewhere you are familiar with can look so new and different in such a situation. Driving through Stromness everything looked so clear and fresh. The lines of the buildings were sharper. The air seemed crisper. People had a new verve about them. The shops seemed more active and interesting. The little cats had more purpose to their daily errands.

Maybe we had left later than usual and life had sparked off, but perhaps it was a greater awareness of detail; an 'after shock'. A wave here, a nod there. It must have been later, for Sigrid gave Borek a wave as he unlocked his shop and there was a long queue issuing from Fletts Butcher.

I think it is that when you are under a great threat, your senses become clearer. Little things assume a different perspective; the stages of the fields showing a seasonal progress. Pigeons flying from stubble. The world going on around you. Seeing these things enforces you to go on and live.

Diana turned up for glazing tuition at three minutes past ten. We got ready to start. A Czech visitor to Orkney, firmly intent on discussing the historic path of the Runic Alphabet passing through Poland, and its relationship with ancient Tibetan Tongues needed attention. I threw pots, demonstrated and listened, whilst bending an ear to Diana's needs and giving her instructions. "This is the way things are," I thought. People have needs, and at times they are multiple.

Sigrid noticed our friend Shayla arriving, so she went out to greet our Hawaiian visitor. Shayla of course asked "Well! How are you guys?" This is when Sigrid cracked up.

They went into the privacy of our pottery loo. Sigrid told Shayla of our plight. Of course she was very alarmed for us and consoling.

As it happened, Shayla was a Cancer Carer in Hawaii for many years; her methods concerned diet, emotion, mineral use, herbs and plenty other things. We however, were not to be overwhelmed by too much information overload. She went back to Ramsquoy where she was staying and returned with some fluids and powders.

This was like a very thin, cold, soup; it was made from powdered herbs and was designed to help cleanse the body by drinking it. She told us that the recommended dose was "Three litres a day!"

I drank the insipid concoction. We were told that the powders were called "Inner Light". If I was to drink this regularly, it would help and strengthen me. "What the Hell!" I thought.

Shayla explained the importance of correct diet according to her methods. It was all getting a bit too much to take in. What she did tell me was, that this in no way replaced the medical profession's advice and methods. What she was telling us was that this was to help me survive the treatment and beat the cancer. I was willing to listen.

Her way would make me stronger and positive. A completely positive attitude was the best weapon in the battle. She also said "Once you have cancer, you always have it. You have it in some shape or form in some of your cells. Therefore, even though the ones we were fighting can be got rid of, the awareness should always be there."

She continued, "even when given the 'all clear,' it could still be danger time. Some patients go into remission and revert to the 'old ways'. This is a No! No! For if you do, a sneaky cancer cell can decide to play tricks on you and grow."

I realised with Sigrid that this would mean a lifetime change in attitude. I will write later about the things I have learned about how you eat. Many of them are so fundamental and simple. It deserves more than just slipping it in here.

I am writing these articles partly to help me understand, but more to help others in the same position, or their friends and families. I won't get everything right, as I am so new to this. I want to share my experiences and talk about Cancer. Some people find it hard to mention the word, or even ask someone who has it, how they are.

Cancer is important to talk about for the sufferer. It acknowledges their plight and they feel relief in talking about it. It helps relieve the stress of their situation, and stress relief is one of the major things which can help a patient.

Shayla told me to keep drinking the 'brew'. She informed me that soon I would have what is called a 'healing crisis'. This would take the form of some reaction and I would feel quite ill. After a few days, this indeed did happen. It came in the form of a really bad attack of gout. It was not pleasant. After feeling so 'weel' I was half crippled. Thankfully I realised that it was the 'crisis' and I continued with the dried weed infusion. Gradually I recovered.

After the weekend Diana and Bob left for Glen Shee and their pottery. We were so glad that they were with us to share our trial. They came to the Cathedral with us to hear the launch of the 'Out of the Stones' CD, which was of Orkney Prehistoric music, and featured the Tomb of the Eagles drums, which I had made. It was very hard to say "on top form" when folk asked how I was. It was a very special experience to be there though, a sense of time and place.

On parting they hoped they had not been in our way. We hugged them and said: "Of course not." We did not know how we would have coped without their sharing friendship"

43 Coping with cancer

'Searching for the primary'

That week we were sent an appointment to attend the Balfour. It was for the X-ray for lung cancer, the colonoscopy and a wee peek down my throat into my stomach.

We were asked to call by two days before, so we could be informed about the examination. This was all very reassuring. I was given a couple of sachets of white powdery stuff to drink. This time I read the instructions carefully. It was the preparation to clear the digestive organs of all matter. I could eat nothing from 7.30pm the evening before I was to attend the inspection of my innards, and I was to take a powder at 7.30am that morning.

The instructions on the packet were simple. Boil some water; pour about half a pint into a large maeasuring jug. Tip the whole contents of said sachet into jug and stir. They didn't say, "Stand well back." I was amazed how the powders exploded!

It was like an experiment by the veritable Professor Beaker from the Muppet Show!

I am very glad that the instructions continued, "Leave for 20 minutes, then stir again and drink all the liquid rapidly."

There were handy tips, too, about being within close proximity to a loo. These I also took heed of wherever I went that day, I kept a weather eye open for the sign of that fit little, blackened ginger bread man, with his legs wide open and feet well apart. (I oft wonder what our prehistoric ancestors would have made of this hieroglyph; someone pegged out in the sand, perhaps as a ritual sacrifice?)

Sigrid took me to the Balfour in the morning. My bowels were clean of all obstructions to clear vision. The three litres of water I had drunk the day before had seen to that, "Running Clear?" as they say. "Like a Mountain stream," I could assure.

I had my X-ray straight away and then was sent to bed. I find the Balfour such a relaxing place to be. I read and slept. There was no thought of work; I was in their control and care. I read and slept again, not worrying about a thing. Well, there were odd moments when apprehension reared itself. I worried about the outcome of the tests and observations. This is when I turned off and went back to my lovely book about an Icelandic farming family in the early 19th Century. I treasured this time to read.

I wondered if hospital would provide more reading time, or, maybe, I could bring Monty, my laptop to hospital and write a bit as well? This thought cheered me no end. (I was missing Monty.)

Lunchtime passed. Of course, I wasn't allowed a morsel. This didn't matter, as the fluid I took to evacuate my bowels must have had a hunger retardant, so I never felt peckish for an instant. "Good dieting stuff," I thought.

Eventually, after several chapters and many naps, I was called for.

My wheelie bed was guided through the corridors to the examination chamber. I could see up the nurse's nose as she steered me to my destination. (I didn't tell her.) There, I was to have more news about the procedures. I asked if they would please go down my throat first, so that the instrument was nice and clean.

They smiled benignly. Dr Dohrn said that I would need an anaesthetic and something else to relax me. "This may give you a peculiar sensation," he said "but don't be embarrassed if you feel you have 'made a mistake.' It is quite normal," he assured me.

I drifted into a blissful sleep, but was rather sorry I couldn't watch the proceedings on the tele screen that they were all privy to observe. Still, I usually nod off at the exciting bit anyway. The search was on for a possible primary cancer, which could have caused the ones in my liver.

I had been told that a primary cancer can be very small and it had to be searched out. The most usual places were the lungs, bowel and stomach; hence all this attention to my abdominal area.

When it was all over I awoke. I was still in the theatre and the staff were doing their duties like a well-disciplined team. I don't know how long it had taken, or who saw what, but I was wheeled back to my space in the Male Ward, supine, but carefully averting my wandering eye from those familiar nasal orifices.

Sigrid arrived and sat on my bedside. She looked great, and told me the news of the day from the pottery. The team of medics arrived and it was 'Curtains' though, thankfully not the terminal ones from American movies; we were surrounded by the private screen. At the end of my bed stood an array of the 'Balfour Brains'. Dr Dohrn told us that the X-rays showed nothing! So 'No' to lung cancer. 'Phew!'

When looking down my throat and into the stomach they found, nothing! 'Phew' number two. (I was assured that they did this first using the unsoiled instrument.) Then, in the expedition up into my bowels; again, nothing! 'Phew' number three, a hatrick perhaps. There were a couple of polyps that they took a biopsy from, just because they were there, sort of thing; 'a bit like a souvenir' I mused, but no horrors to report.

The experts all smiled with genuine pleasure that nothing horrible had turned up. Sigrid and I were very relieved indeed.

I had taken things quite casually, but the undertones of apprehension were always there. It is the not knowing, which is really worrying. At least when you do understand what is wrong, you can deal with it when the time comes. Knowing where you are is a great thing, even if what you have to face up to is uncomfortable. At least that is how I felt about it all.

The good doctor told me that I would now have to go to Aberdeen for a scan. This was to enable a further search to see if there was something lurking where they couldn't see. He would arrange this for me. I would also need a liver biopsy to see what they were really dealing with, and that would indicate my course of treatment.

I was told that I was looking extremely well inside and out. I was very strong and would certainly respond well to their recommendations of chemotherapy. One of the reasons for my current health was that I had been working on dieting through the summer. I hadn't lost weight, but had been working in my own way on a more healthy approach to life.

I had taken up swimming and some relaxation, but what I really think helped me enormously was Shayla's approach to my diet. Here's some of what I learned.

Firstly, I was to drink three litres of pure water daily. This water was to be mixed with the vegetable and herb powders she gave me ... trade name, Inner Light.

The waters should be drunk a litre at a time, three times a day. Each litre should be drunk swiftly, gulped down in fact. It is amazing how you get used to this. This brew would cleanse the body of stored up acids. Your pee would change colour, and of course you would do a lot of it.

After a wee while, like a week, it was likely that I would go through a 'Healing Crisis'. This indeed happened, as I described earlier, it took the form of a prolonged and painful gout attack. We had two dinner parties during this spell of agony. One dinner Sigrid cooked, and the other, our twelfth wedding anniversary do, I prepared. (Recipes later ... much later) This gout attack took a week to subside, and hasn't returned.

Shayla recommended that I continue this drinking for many months, or even forever. I was now used to it and doubled the amount of herby stuff and squeezed the juice of a fresh lemon in every two litres. If I woke in the early hours, I took a litre then, as it should not be drunk near food times. It actually helped me go back to sleep, and initially, I could feel my veins tingle through my body, as if my blood was being cleaned.

Next week I will write about the diet I am on and why. It is not easy, but I realise the sheer sense of it.

If I can explain it, I hope it can be of help to other potential cancer patients. There are important implications for everybody, healthy or no. So, if you can wait, please do, and read next week's Orkney Today.

Yours, Aye, and forever ... Andrew

44 Coping with cancer

'Smacking the baby'

With the threat of cancer, one experiences 'highs' and 'lows'. This episode was written during a 'high' period. Do enjoy it.

Our friend, Shayla Spencer, from Hawaii, was a cancer care specialist for many years. She now only helps friends. We feel fortunate to know her. I have explained how she gave me the green herbs to drink in a litre of water three times a day. This I found, and still find very important.

I certainly felt very well, despite what the doctors thought. In fact they asked me why I was feeling so well. I am certainly not saying they are a miracle cure, it may well be all in the mind, but if it works, don't knock it. The sheer cleansing effect alone of drinking all that fluid must be good, if only for the kidneys.

An absolutely fundamental thing, which Shayla mentioned, was: "A cancer is like a baby! Only this baby will kill you if you feed it!" She went on in full flow "So! Babies like 'Baby food.' Well! Just cut out all the things that will make a baby grow; these are all milk products. Milk should only be used for feeding babies, not adults! So that means cheese, butter, cream, ice cream and anything with milk or cream in it!"

"But I love cheeses and cream sauces." I winced. Shayla explained to me, "and that's just what your baby inside you wants; when it doesn't get its milky way, it will cry and crave. Smack that baby!" She said. "Don't give it the cream, deny it the cheese."

Actually, it wasn't a real hardship, just cream in chowder, Orkney Vanilla Ice Cream with Cointreau, Camembert, Brie and Farm cheese. I remember them fondly as "Old Friends". I have made new friends now, and they like me. Apples, pears, grapes, nectarines and peaches

136

are my new buddies.

Feeding this wretched "Baby" also meant eggs and anything to do with them. Eggs will form into chicks. So goodbye caviar?" I questioned. "So long! Caviar" Shayla waved. "Ah well! There's always beetroot" I sighed. "Right on!" she encouraged. "Beetroot's very good for you." "Don't I just know that," I thought inwardly. However, I was certain that this was all for the best.

Alcohol, too, is just a passing fancy now, only a little red wine, and not every day. This, I thought would be the hard one, but no. If it is necessary, then do it. Treating cancer has to be done in a business like manner; Emotions are important, but so is keeping a clear head.

The other thing, which Shayla insisted on, was that I should find out my blood type. This was essential, because with the aid of a book called 'Eat Right For Your Type' by Dr Peter J D'Adamo (ISBN 0-7126-7716-X) –Available from Tam's Bookshop, Stromness – I could get a diet which would further de-tox me and help me lose weight in the correct way. I would also gain strength and feel fitter and stronger.

Finding out your blood type is not so simple. It should be easy though. Luckily for me it was, I nipped in and asked Dr Hazleshurt if he would kindly liberate a modest amount for testing. This is not a normal procedure for the National Health Service. [I think it should be.] We have a right to know what our blood type is. It is a very useful thing to have, as it sometimes comes up in conversation, well, it does now; lots in fact.

Syringe and swabs in hand, my physician made a beeline for my letting vein. The minor extraction was made and the sample secreted in a wee packet for despatch to the Hospital lab.

A couple of days later I rang in to enquire after the health of the spider plants and the begonias in the Dounby surgery's waiting arena. "All well," I heard. Then a familiar voice came through the telegraph, "AB Positive". "Sure?" I queried. "Positive!" then an afterthought: "Any left over for Black Puddings?"

Of course, I had to be the rare blood group, didn't I. Apparently, my group has only been around for about a thousand years, so Julius Caesar and I don't have much in common. The point of all this, though, is, each blood group requires a selected diet. There are some things, which are good for one group and bad for another. Hence the old adage, "One man's meat is another man's poison."

I can't, here, go through all the things, just a few odd examples. For AB Positive, no chicken, geese or ducks, but turkey is ok occasionally.

No beef or pork, but sheep, goats and venison are fine (We've just stocked up with North Ronaldsay mutton. Yum! Yum!) No haddock, but cod is beneficial. No crab or lobster, but scallops and mussels are good; you see, it isn't too bad. I can have chicken livers and calves liver, but not their hosts {or hostesses}. One of the reasons is that AB+ has lower levels of stomach acid, so it deals differently with certain foods. This reflects in one's health and well-being.

Sigrid offered to stop eating some of the many things we were previously able to enjoy together. I asked her this. "My dear sweetheart, if I had a broken leg, would you go around wearing my plaster for me?". "No!" She answered. "Well then" I said, "you just carry on enjoying the things you want, and I am sure I won't starve. In any case, you like cod and lamb and scallops, so it will all be alright you'll find"

Shayla visited. To be really healthy I had cooked spoots in our French iron pot, by laying them on top of some fresh asparagus and simmering for only a few minutes. They were excellent.

I served white wine and I had bought a great pack of sparkling mineral water for me. "No!" Shayla exclaimed. "That water is pumped full of carbon dioxide, just what cancers love." She explained that cancers did not grow easily with a well oxygenated blood supply, therefore, all sparkly drinks were a severe "No! No!" She added: "Except of course for champagne and good sparkling wines" "Phew!" I uttered as I mopped my brow. This all made sense to me. The right kind of bubbles!

Shayla continued on about carbon. "All burnt foods, char grills, burnt roasted vegetables, smoked foods, crusty and scorched pizzas, these all put carbon into the bloodstream. So, No! Andrew. This is the way to curb the cancers and reduce their power."

Whilst Shayla was on the subject of carbon, she explained why fried food is so bad for cancer prone people. "To fry food", she said, "you have to heat the oil or fat. This changes the oil as it burns in the heating process; this burning creates carbon, and you eat it. Thus from fried food you put more carbon into your bloodstream." Just think of the list of fried things that we can stuff ourselves with, try this…. Crisps, chips, pop corn, bacon sandwiches, burgers, and doughnuts. I shan't go on. (Anything in batter) Sad isn't it, but true.

Just to go one step further. "Sugar!!" Bad for everybody. Well! I don't have a sweet tooth anyway.

There is a world of other things to eat and drink. I will give a very positive view of this later, and how things work out for me.

45 Coping with cancer

'Clan Haven'

IT seemed forever, waiting to get news of when I was going to have my scan to check for a primary cancer that was meant to be hidden away somewhere. I was told that it was extremely rare to get two primaries in one organ.

My liver seemed to support two areas of trouble, so these had to stem from somewhere. My X rays, showed nothing in my lungs, and the delve into my bowels and stomach showed clear.

I visited Dr Frost, partly to indicate that I did not show 'favouritism' in the Dounby Health Centre. He reckoned that after my scan and a liver biopsy, it would be a couple of weeks before the results would be through. Therefore, he told me, we could go to our house in France for a holiday, then come home to Orkney and commence my proposed treatment. I had an excellent conversation with him about Chemotherapy. I was very fit, quite young and, for once, absolutely healthy. I could therefore stand really heavy doses of Chemo, and my cure would be quicker. He also agreed that the "alternative treatment" I was undergoing was perfectly fine, in fact beneficial. His one proviso was that I still took the recommended established treatment. This, I was going to do as I thought that the one aided the other.

Sigrid and I decided to make our plans. She was to go away first. Her 'duties' were to gather our crop of walnuts, get the garden tidied up, (an everlasting occupation), make the house ready and have a nice time. She was also to tell our friends about my cancer problem; we had lost a dear potter friend, Jean-Pierre the year before to this scourge, so it would not be easy for them hearing our news. I was to join her shortly after my biopsy. (Man plans: God laughs).

Dr Dohrn was to see me on October 17. I jotted him a wee note to say it would be good to have my scan and biopsy before then. Thus the appointment at Aberdeen somehow got nudged on, even though there was no bed for me. I had to be there on the day Sigrid left for France. We ended going our separate ways, Sigrid on the "Ola" at 06.30, me off to the Airport for the early flight.

It was very strange arriving at the hospital. Oncology, Ward 15. I had never thought I would be a cancer victim, but then, probably most folk don't think that either. We are often in denial. I had a large and heavy bottle of my green drink to take, hospital or no, I was having it! I was to see Dr Louise Murray. She is young, petite, and kind. I had a good book, so the waiting wasn't too bad.

Dr Lou concurred with my previous medics about my prognosis. This wasn't easy for me, and possibly for her too, as she added that in my case, surgery wasn't an option. It was strange that I felt so well, but here I was, in a cancer ward. I knew that I had to be POSITIVE. She remarked on my attitude, and my vast bottle of Green Drink. Then I was given a White Drink to take; this was to show up all my innards for the scan that I was to have the next day. The ward Sister apologised for having no bed for me. I didn't mind, as I wasn't an invalid yet. I was staying at Clan Haven, nearby. I knew nothing about it, and was to find out.

A 60p bus ride town-wards took me to Clan Haven. This is an old, impressive, granite church building on a forked junction close to town. I tried the Haven door; it was shut. I wandered round the edifice in a lost, timid way. I was unsure about everything. I found cars parked there, so I assumed someone was about. Further round I came across a large, glazed portal, I opened that door, and was ushered in through another. "Mr Appleby, we've been expecting you." I was so relieved. These were real people. They greeted me and I was shown around Clan House. I was told that the place was set up for cancer patients, their friends and relatives. Upstairs there was a library, an IT room and spaces to sit and study or just be.

On the ground floor was a large area with the sound of running water. This came from a lovely rock pool to one side. You could sit and just watch. There was a cafeteria, meeting rooms, and a sales area to help fund 'CLAN'. There were people with cancer, friends, helpers, and family. A great sense of well-being and positivism pervaded the whole place.

I was shown through to where I was to stay. I was so pleased, there was an excellent kitchen I could use, 'Hooray, I could self-cater,' I had everything. There was a special fridge for chemotherapy patients and another for others. There were breakfast cereals, milk and fruit juices. What is more, a happy atmosphere. This whole place was so well and thoughtfully designed for cancer care and support. I wasn't alone. I was shown my room, an en-suite single with tele and kettle, just like a Holiday Inn, only better. I was given a code for the Clan door, the one that was shut earlier. Now it was my door.

Well! I just had to go shopping. I got mis-directed to a Sainsbury's and ended up at a Marks and Sparks. Never mind, I found a brilliant Lebanese restaurant, called Genaro's, on the way, which was to become my regular haunt. I bought lots of fresh veg at Marks, rice, nuts, fruit, olive oil, garlic. All the lovely things my healthy side craved. On the way back, I settled into the homely Lebanese place and had Lamb Kebabs and rice. It was so good, and only cost £4.60. I had green tea too. The décor was plain, the cutlery simple, the crockery ordinary, the food ... Excellent!!

Next day at 9am, I was due for my scan. I had taken another white preparation at 7.20am to "Show me up." I was given a bed, even though I didn't want to use it, "I wasn't ill – yet." I mused. I looked round the ward and asked myself "Am I one of them?" I was new to this. It was hard to come to terms with. One day, up, another, down.

I was offered a wheel chair to be taken to the Radiology Dept. I said, " I can walk just fine"-+- "As you like" the porter returned. He took me, unaided, to the scan. Fully dressed I was admitted. The nice radiographer ushered me to lie down on the couch after removing my top-clothes. As I lay there I looked at the lovely picture of an idyllic country scene. {I hoped this wasn't "Soylan Green"} Anyway, I pointed up to it and asked the kind Doctor if he could see the pigeon in the tall tree depicted above us. "No." he remarked as he peered upwards. "Ah! It's just crapped in your eye!!" I was pleased to inform him. He jerked back and reached for a tissue. "What fun!" I thought.

The scan was just like a great Polo Mint going round me. It wasn't like a scary coffin thing. Some folk are worried about it, but it's OK. Just watch for the pigeons and close your eyes when told to. It was all over soon and the radiographer thanked me for my visit. "I loved the messy dickey-bird bit," he admitted.

I was to get my scan results the following day, I was told, but would have to return for my biopsy another time. "Blast!" I thought. This would put paid to my trip to France with Sigrid.

'MAN PLANS: GOD LAUGHS.'

I had two nights at Clan Haven. I met so many positive people, and felt the great warmth of the place. 'Orkney Today,' is there each week, as are 'The Orcadian' and 'Shetland Times.' There are also so many other reminders for us Island folk, who require Clan Haven's wonderful facilities and support.

Dr Hazlehurst

46 Coping with cancer

'The biopsy'

Flying back from Aberdeen, Clan Haven and my little Lebanese restaurant, I had time to reflect on the news. Surgery was not an option as the assumed cancers were too spread through my liver.

My chances lay in my own will power, positivity and chemotherapy. This would mean a prolonged period of sickness due to my proposed treatment. This was a worry indeed. Also there was the risk of infections due to reduced immunity, the tiredness and lethargy that would be another by-product of my predicament. All these things had to be taken into account. So I began to plan.

Going to France for the winter was out. Potting for the winter was not going to work, but I could write. I enjoy writing; I could spend my time pursuing this new development. Maybe the book that has been within me could emerge. I have begun it, but it needs lots of time and thought. This became my resolve. Monty, my faithful laptop, was with me on the plane, and I had been writing some of this series in hospital and at Clan Haven.

Monty could come to the Macmillan Ward and be my pen and paper pal. I had been watching people in hospital reading magazines and viewing television. I would write and try to be creative. This was my plan hatching.

Arriving home was a comfort. Barbel Dister, a potter from Cromarty and her husband Colin were staying in our wee hoose, Sigrid was in France though. This was Friday evening. My daughter Ruth and her husband Mark were arriving that Saturday evening, just after Barbel and Colin were going home. A quick turn around indeed!

My news wasn't so good, and Sigrid was regretting being away, but that was how it panned out. It was not going to be an option for me to go away to France myself now, as my biopsy had not been done. I accepted my lot.

Barbel and Colin arrived back after visiting Babbette in South Ronaldsay. It was good to see them. We chatted about life and then to bed. I slept well. In the morning, about 7.21am, I got up. The whole room spun round and I fell against the wall. I lay on my bed and shook. It was hard getting up again. The giddiness returned. I made for the stairs and got to the loo.

Everything was spinning round. I recovered a little and called for Barbel. "I'm ill." I told her. She and Colin helped me back up to bed. I had never felt like that before. The rafters in our room revolved rapidly. "Was this the cancer setting in?" I wondered. I had been asked by the doctors if I had had dizzy spells ever. "No" had been my answer.

I decided to ride this one out for a day or two. Ruth would be here soon. Colin rigged up a Phone for me by my bed. I could then phone and be phoned without shifting. I contacted Shayla who arrived. I felt very lucky to have such folk at hand.

Shayla thought that I might have had a blood sugar deficiency, so she made me a special drink. It helped, but I wasn't fit to go about yet. Then she taught me a mantra for relaxation and meditation. It went "SSSeeeeeeeee" on the inward breath and "HhAAaaaaaaaaaRRRMmmm" on the outward breath.

I could vary the length of these sounds according to my feelings. As I concentrated on this and repeated it audibly to myself, I fell into a deep and relaxed slumber. Shayla told me that I would need to do this twice a day for 20 minutes at least. This meditative mantra would help me in relaxation, which was very good for aiding recovery from Cancer and in its treatment. I use it often now.

I was settled, so Barbel and Colin could go on the lunchtime ferry. Shayla had commitments that afternoon, but I felt ok to be left alone. I rested and slept until late afternoon. Sigrid and I chatted on the phone; this helped us both, even though it was an alarming situation. Were these to be my first real symptoms? Hard to say! ... I elected not to call my good doctor. Not yet.

At about five pm. I thought I'd better do something positive. Ruth and Mark, with their two 'Staffy' doggies were arriving on the evening ferry. I decided to get up and cook. I got spinach pasta from the Stromness Deli and prepared a large 'veggy' dinner for us, with loads of garlic, aubergines, onion and a thickened tomato sauce. This was all on my AB+ diet and simple to do. The chopping, slicing and preparing of this was a form of meditation in itself. It occupied me and steadied me. When Mark and Ruth arrived, all was easy.

We could enjoy a Sunday and then it was the meeting with Dr. Dohrn on the Monday at Mid-day. I wanted Ruth to come with me so that she was "up to speed" with everything.

I heard it all again, and it was good for Ruth to understand.

Yes! My liver cancers were treatable with chemotherapy, but not surgery. Arrangements would be made for my return to Aberdeen for the biopsy and another look into my bowels at a "swelling" on its lining. Could this be the elusive primary cancer? Another look, another biopsy. We would only be there for one day and a night. A peer up my insides in the morning, a liver biopsy in the afternoon, plane home next day; simple. (Man plans, God laughs.)

We were to go down on the Wednesday to the Aberdeen Royal Infirmary. To get things well organised, we got the enema powders from the Balfour, so I could take the first lot on Tuesday night, then, the second instalment on Wednesday morning, leaving time for "evacuation" before getting on the plane.

The plan would have worked, but I had a call from the surgery on Monday evening. Would I be able to fly down on Tuesday lunchtime, as the doctors in Aberdeen wanted me there earlier? I agreed to go with Ruth then, so we booked accommodation at Clan Haven and packed quickly. We had to collect our tickets from Dounby Health Centre just after 9.03am. We did this and then completed several tasks at the pottery. The giddiness had subsided and now only occurred when I got up or went to bed, maybe just an inner ear problem, which was mending. I hoped so.

I had advanced the self-administration of the wicked enema powders so that I was clear for the hospital probings.

I was to be quite ready for them. We flew off on time; no in-flight snack for me. The courtesy bus got us to hospital rapidly, and we reached ward 15 just after 2.17pm. Dr Louise Murray was amazed; we had made it! I told her that I was fully prepared and starved for the look up my rear.

Biopsy – Part Two. Next week. If you can bear it.

47 Coping with cancer

'The biopsy – part 2'

This too, was Ruth's first visit to a cancer ward. She saw, as I had the week before, what was in store for me at Aberdeen Royal Infirmary, and was going to help me through this next stage. Dr Louise was impressed that we had done all the 'delicious' bowel preparations. However, I was only there early for the blood tests, she told us.

These were a series of extractions taken from one puncture into a good, throbbing vein. The first syringe went in, and plasma was sucked out into a wee, transparent cartridge. This capsule was then unscrewed and a further one inserted. This withdrawing of blood was repeated several times.

I asked why, and for what this was being done. I didn't mind about it, but I think it is always a good idea to enquire. There is sometimes a chance of learning something, isn't there?

The petite Dr Murray explained, "We want to know how well your blood clots, Andrew." Then she continued, "If we know this, we will have an advantage if there is an emergency." I felt that a further question was due from me. "What kind of emergency?" "A very rare one, Andrew. This is purely a precaution. We may cause bleeding in your liver, if your blood clots well, then all will be fine. If, however it doesn't, then we have to be ready for that." This was a reasonable argument, and I was happy with this learning curve.

I wasn't due for the colonoscopy that afternoon, I was told, so Ruth and I could leave. The sister gave me an extra dose of purgative for the morn. She said "Now, don't eat anything, only take liquids. Soup, maybe, but only clear." She added "We need you to be running clear so we can get a good view." They agreed we could go to Clan Haven for the night and return at 09.05 am for my inner view.

I was glad to bring Ruth to Clan, where we were going to stay. This is the cancer haven for patients, family and friends. We had packed a selection of Fursbreck's products for their Christmas Market, as the funding for this superb establishment is largely by their own efforts. We had a twin room, en-suite. Clan Haven is a real haven. We all know what we are undergoing here. This brings such understanding, help and support from those who are staying there with us.

It seems that there is always someone who can help, or be helped. It makes you feel that even when you have cancer, you are a real person and not a victim. From this you can gather positive strength and a sense of the future. When you have this, then you can understand more and even help others.

Some folk shy away from cancer; this is a form of denial. The person with it must be able to talk about it and be asked about it. They need to be faced and asked how they are. The word CANCER has to be used by the enquirer and also the host of that disease. The person with cancer can then speak freely, thus releasing inner tensions they may have.

Stress can assist cancer to spread and grow. Talking about it, sometimes even in a casual way, is such a help and release for the afflicted. This is why Clan Haven is so brilliant.

I was not able to eat that afternoon, or evening. I was fasting. Ruth was not. We went to the lovely Lebanese restaurant where she had lamb kebab, followed by one of the best honey crepes that I have ever witnessed. For me, spring water. It was a pleasure, though, to watch her enjoy her repast. I don't know what the waiter thought about this, but that doesn't matter, does it!

I allowed myself a glass of wine with Ruth on the way back to Clan. On returning, I wrote and she did business things. The morning would see the colonoscopy and the biopsy soon enough. The calm of Clan ensured deep sleep. The purgative, which was prescribed, must have an appetite suppressant, for there were no hunger pangs to waken me in the night.

We turned up at ARI at 8.33am. This time I was put to bed. We were offered tea and biscuits, but I declined. Later, I found out that there was to be no colonoscopy, just the biopsy, so I had starved for two days for nothing. Well! I was on a diet anyway, so what the matter, tomorrow's another ... fast!

I was given a really special drink that would make everything inside me show up; then a kindly young doctor ran me through the consent form. He must have been very well trained in presenting this. It all sounded quite pleasant, except for the bit about piercing my vital organs with a 'foreign body' and the possible risk of infection.

I was in their hands and signed the papers trustingly. He assured me, though, that the instruments they were going to stick into me were actually quite sterile. I was only to have a local anaesthetic and would be wide-awake through the whole process. I joke about it, but this was serious business as far as I was concerned.

I was trollyed away in my wheelie bed to the wee theatre several lift stops below. Ruth stayed outside. I admired the doctor's green apron who was going to perform the deep feat within me. She was delighted, as she was Irish, and it was her favourite emerald hue. We looked together at the ultra-sound screen.

Here, I too could visualise what we were up against. Centrally placed, right amongst some major blood vessels was a big dark mark. There were other lesions and tiny highlights spread about therein.

The lightsome Irish doctor had to make a very difficult choice. Most of the affected parts were too peedie to get a decent sample from, so the only real option was to aim for the big one. (I was told earlier that there were two large and serious areas.)

The discussion went like this. "I will need one of the very fine biopsy needles." I asked: "Why?" "Because, one of the huge, fat ones could easily puncture one of your big blood vessels." I asked limply: "Is this dangerous?" {Actually meaning the tumour} She answered: "Yes! One slip and there's a problem." Then I queried abstractedly, "The actual tumour? Is that able to be treated?" "Oh! Yes. Once the biopsy is over and we have a good sample, then we will be able to determine what sort of treatment and how much chemo-therapy you will need." She added: "The danger is piercing your deep blood vessels."

I was actually relieved. All we needed now was a successful biopsy with no accidents. I was given a local anaesthetic and the needle was being aimed at the offending dark lump nestling around my blood channels. I elected not to watch the needle's progress on the monitor. Instead I said and repeated the mantra that Shayla had taught me "SEEEEEEeeeeeee HHHAAAAAaaaaaMMMmmmm" I could feel the pressure within me and some pain. The mantra helped. The pressure stopped. The doctor said: "I've missed. We will have to

go in once more" Again I didn't watch the screen. I mantraed on...
"SSSSSEEEEeeeee hhHHHHaaaaAAAAAmmmMMMM."(The
mantra can change with your will and mood.)

I was offered more local anaesthetic. "Yes.," I replied "but only if
you can spare it." "Plenty yet." somebody answered. Another needle
came my way, followed by the second fine biopsy instrument. The
thoughtful lady doctor told me "I am now hoping for a good sample,
but fine needles don't always achieve that." I admired her frankness.
Inward and downward progressed the second attempt. The pain
began again as the point passed the range of the anaesthetic. My
mantra continued.

"Too Short!!" I heard. "The needle's too short!! We will have to go
in again." There was a hurried search for a third needle. The search
was getting longer. I absent-mindedly wondered about Woollie's
knitting counter, then decided to go on with my mantra and behave.
I was offered some extra anaeesthetic. "Merci," I uttered. I enjoyed
the levity of the moment. It relieved the tension. I know it was very
difficult and worrying indeed for the doctor in charge.

48 Coping with cancer

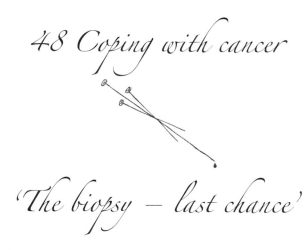

'The biopsy – last chance'

The biopsy needle was aimed, hopefully for a direct hit this time. This must be highly skilled work indeed. The pressure below my ribs increased as the pain began again. The mantra helped enormously. Whenever I was asked to breathe very gently, I could. If required to hold breath, it was easy. I was able also to think past any pain and remain in control of my feelings. I was actually in a calm relaxed state, but very aware.

For a few remaining moments I was advised to keep extremely still. I thought to myself: "Well! I'm not going anywhere at the mo anyway, am I?"

I could feel the sheer tension around the ultrasound screen as that biopsy needle was reaching its target: ever closer to the tumour, and ever nearer those vital arteries. "Keep very, very still Mr. Appleby." "Mmmmmmmmmmm" I thought, as the pressure began to increase and then slowly, slowly ease. I don't know whether there was a slight twisting feeling or not from deep in my liver. It was almost as if there was something being gripped? Maybe it was my imagination, but moments after this sensation someone said "PHEW!!" Others sighed.

The biopsy ordeal was past. I heard, in an Irish lilt thus, "Turrd time lucky!" I opened my eyes to a relieved doctor with an emerald green apron on … with no bloodstains. "Right! That's it. We've done it." A male voice concurred. "All finished?" I ventured. "Yes! And what was that you were wheezing out?" I heard, while some rubber gloves snapped off. "Just my mantra. Want to hear it again?" "No!" "OK."

"Now! Mr Appleby," I heard, "you must lie absolutely still for six hours," the kind voice continued, "This is to stop any chance of bleeding from the wounds to your liver." I kept supine and immobilised as my bed was being wheeled back to Ward 15. I decided to avoid the view up the porter's nostrils in case I laughed. (Last laugh perhaps.)

Ruth, my daughter, was walking next to me as I gazed up to the passing ceiling. How I wished there were a few paintings on it to relieve its dullness.

We arrived back and played 'I Spy.' My field of vision was limited, so there had to be boundaries. 'Condensation' was one of the things, 'Interstice,' another. 'Gossamer' took ages to guess as did 'Fissure.' I read from the book about John Rae, 'Fatal Passage', (apt, I thought). Crosswords and a horizontal snooze passed the hours. Six of these hours later, exactly, I got up for a pee. I didn't collapse in a pool of blood in the loo, so I felt that I'd got through it all.

I was given poached haddock with tatties and peas, some fruit salad and a cup of tea. "Food," I thought. Then I was given a dose more of that enema fluid and a load more for the morning. "Faecal Passage," I thought, as we were permitted to go back to Clan Haven. I took the ravenous Ruth to the lovely Lebanese restaurant; I merely as an onlooker while she had a beautiful aubergine and lamb tajine supper. I made a few discreet trips to the loo.

I drank plenty of water that night as the hospital staff wanted me 'running clear' for a better view. Ruth toasted for breakfast while I took my last litre of clear, clean water. When we reached the hospital at 08 47 the staff in Ward 15, asked how I was "doing." "Clear as a mountain stream," I related. Their approval was graciously received. My appointment was fixed. I would be the first! I found out I would only be the first in the afternoon, though.

Midday arrived, and the afternoon hadn't begun at ARI. At 1.23pm. it still hadn't started. We began to mutter, because we were booked on the afternoon flight back. This left at 5.30, the bus left ARI at 3.02pm. I had to be done, dusted and dressed.

Finally we were directed to the X-ray department and a wee area where we were to wait for the colonoscopy examination. It was nearly 2pm when they remarked, "Why hadn't I said I was waiting." I explained I had been saying that for three days now. Then, the gowned gathering started to speak about all the time I had spent waiting and what could have been done about it. I interrupted politely thus: "we are here, now. Our plane goes at 5.30pm. The coach will leave at 3pm. Please, let's get on with the here and now." "Good idea," they agreed, then added, "but, Andrew, you have to have an hour to get over the anaesthetic." I asked, "What Anaesthetic?" "The one you have to have, to get through this of course!" I merely repeated, "What Anaesthetic?"

They got the gist of it. There was a huddle. The grimness of physicians then informed me: "Where we want to look is a long way up. It could be painful." I thought for a second. I knew Ruth was desperate to get back to her husband, Mark. They had arrived on holiday, and Ruth had spent her time with me in Aberdeen and not with her man. He was going to have to return to teach the next day. Ruth wanted to see him. I repeated, "NO ANAESTHETIC, thank you."

It was Vanessa from Stenness who got the probes ready. She was a good friend of Pauline who lived at the Harray Post Office. They used to pop round to the pottery from time to time. Here she was now, administering to my 'nethers'. It is amazing how one catches up with things, isn't it? I had an excellent view of the ultrasound screen, and this time I wasn't going to miss a moment. It became all quite good fun really. Up, up and up the tubey bits went. The little camera on its end was showing us the innerscape of my abdomen.

To avoid any discomfort and to relax myself, I repeated my mantra "SSSSSeeeeeeee HHHhhhhAAAaaaaammmm". In due time the probe reached its destination. There, growing from the side of my intestines was a small tumour. Was this the primary? It looked just like a Turkish Sultan's hat. It was actually a very pretty thing: STRIPED AND ONION SHAPED, THERE IT WAS. I WAS LOOKING AT MY ENEMY. This was a good thing. I could see it; therefore, I knew what to fight, pretty though it was.

The chief Doc took a biopsy. I could see the wee instruments plucking bits away. I could only just feel a dull sensation deep in the tum. All were watching. This was far more gripping even than the Moon Landing. For me, a last look at the wee 'Turk's headgear' as the camera receded. The tubes were being retracted and I could watch it all in speedy reverse. It felt really quite wiggly inside my guts.

In a few moments all was withdrawn and I was able to move again. Ruth had rushed up to the cancer ward and retrieved my gear. I dressed and we made for the airport bus, waving a "cheerio" to the theatre staff.

The transport had left ages before. We grabbed a taxi and sped off. The driver needed petrol so we delayed for eleven minutes while he flooded his tank. We had to be there an hour before, and time was close. The British Airways check-in had a short queue of nine folk. We got to the head of it fairly rapidly. We showed our tickets. Gloria, the check-in maiden, announced: "The flight's closed, it leaves at four thirty, not five thirty." It was four twenty two. Ruth got her arguing face into gear. "I need to get back. My husband's waiting for me. He leaves tomorrow and I have to see him." She went on, "there must be a seat left."

Gloria told her: "The flight is very full, Mrs Colston." Ruth replied, "The word 'Very' means not quite!" Gloria phoned. I must say how well she coped. She actually quoted Ruth's qualification of that word, 'very'. The Taxiing of the aircraft was halted. Gloria then added: "But YOUR ticket, Mr Appleby has been CANCELLED. You will have to go back to the hospital." The amount of times I said "NING" under my breath.

I caught Ruth's rear view charging through security. I waited so see if she was ejected from the flight. No! She'd made it.

49 Coping with cancer

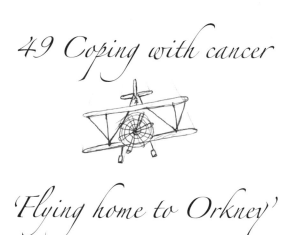

'Flying home to Orkney'

I made my way back to Aberdeen Royal Infirmary to ward 15. It was being closed for the weekend. The Sister was surprised to see me, so too was her able assistant. I explained my predicament and they were very kind in advising me what to do.

As we chatted about things that go wrong, the nice assistant (I never did get her name) said: "Well! Mr Appleby. The good news is that the tumour they found in your upper bowel is non-malignant."

I was amazed. The result was so quick. I suppose that officially I wasn't to know for a while yet, but I wasn't upset by the early news.

I was told the procedure to reinstate my flight ticket in the morning, so I was delighted to advance to Clan Haven for the night. The thought of the Lebanese restaurant didn't disturb me too much either. I still had plenty of my 'Inner Light' herbal drink to last me, so all was very well. It was only the bruising from the liver biopsy that was a discomfort, even that, though, was subsiding.

I was very glad to return to Clan Haven. There, I could feel quite at home. I had my room back and set up 'Monty' my laptop, got out my books 'Say No To Cancer' and 'Diet 4 Life.'

Round one had been won at the Balfour, no lung cancer. Round two was bowel cancer, but that had to be replayed at Aberdeen Royal Infirmary. Round three was the complete scan at ARI. Nothing was found. It was now down to round four, the biopsy results. I knew that would be ten to twelve days. I chose to go into 'denial' and get on with life and work. I was not, however, going to neglect my dieting and cancer fighting tactics.

In the morning I got an early taxi to the airport and then the first plane back to Orkney. It was so good to get home. There was even an ember glowing from Ruth and Mark's coal fire from the night before. There was a note to say they were out playing on the beach, so all was well. I went to the Pottery. Annabelle had been covering for us while we were away and the mail was neatly piled for me to go through. Sigrid was flying back from France soon, so life was all in place.

I felt very content at that time. I had done the best I could at making my arrangements for the future. This included checking and amending insurance policies, making plans for my occupations during chemotherapy and calming myself over the prospect of not really doing any potting for several months. That was the hard bit, but the chance to have time to write allowed me to look forward, in a way, to the future.

Ruth, my daughter, needed lots of pottery for her shop. She and her husband Mark were going to drive down with it to North Berwick. This now wasn't to be. We were packing it for posting instead, and that was boring work.

I said to Ruth: "Rooooth, I've got a better plan. Why don't we pack my van and I drive us to North Berwick and we can pick up Sigrid at the same time?"

"A good plan, Dad." That was Sunday. We left on the Monday's early boat.

The drive took us past my brother Malcolm's golden domain, then to Edinburgh for Sigrid, a swift trip to IKEA for herrings and candles, then to Ruth and Mark. Mark had cooked a great fish dish. He had adopted the 'Diet 4 Life' blood group philosophy. His energy levels were considerably up, and he was feeling even better than usual. Next day we enjoyed visiting Ruth's high street pottery shop. Sigrid was most impressed, it being her first visit.

Thence we went to stay with old friends, Robert and Audrey. Robert, in his sprightly early eighties, had recently been operated on for liver cancer. His op, though straightforward, wasn't without risks. He was recovering very well. Their little doggie, Ben, was my foot doctor from before. He was the wiry Jack Russell who once licked my athlete's feet back to health. He gave me a 'booster' licking, and I managed to get some photos of this toe job.

It was good to have a couple of days away. It was my wee holiday. On our return it had to be back to reality again. At least a few days had passed and we were closer to those awaited biopsy results. The normal routine of life took over.

A couple of days slipped by, and we had really forgotten all about cancer.

We were working away at the pottery, and I had just come in from plucking a few teal when the phone rang. Sigrid handed it to me.

"It's the Hospital," she whispered, as she handed me the receiver.

"Dr Louise Murray here, from the ARI". I gulped. She continued, "It's about your biopsy results." I clutched the handset harder, "Yes," I registered.

Dr Murray went on: "the problem, Andrew, is that it is all getting very puzzling. We know that we got to the right place in your liver, even though it was difficult. I have to tell you that the results show only positively healthy liver tissue."

I was amazed. I replied, "Isn't that good?"

"Well, yes," she ventured. Then she asked me this: "how are you feeling?"

"Well!" I said, "very well indeed."

The doctor then remarked: "could it be that horrible looking green stuff you drink all the time?"

"Probably!" was my answer.

Dr M then spelled it out to me what was going to happen next. She said: "we are going to have a high level conference all about you next Monday."

"I can't wait," I intervened.

She explained further: "we will look through all your X-rays, slides, biopsies and other tests. Then it may mean you returning for a further examination afterwards, just to make sure. I shall ring you back in about a week's time."

"Thank you Doctor, and I'll just carry on with the green stuff, will I?"

"Yes! Keep up the GREENS, Andrew." The phone clicked.

Sigrid and I got on with our lives again. Pots had to be made and sent out. Dinners had to be cooked. Washing up done. 'Normal' life ensued. Our cancer care went on just the same, but you see, this had become normal to us. We were careful all the time over our diet and the way we lived and did things.

So, time went by, and the week elapsed. Forgetful of the awaited phone call, we simply carried on. Then the bell tolled.

"Ahem! Dr Louise Murray here."

I stopped my silly voice and answered seriously.

"Well! Andrew. We have had our conflab, and there was a lot of thought and research about your case. We have now come up with the diagnosis."

I trembled as Sigrid listened to my side of the conversation. "What do you think, then?"

"You have what is called a haemangeoma!"

"What's that?"

Nice Dr. Murray explained, "It is like a lot of hardened blood in your liver. It resembles a birthmark. It is non malignant, not cancer, and we at the Aberdeen Royal Infirmary are extremely happy for you—."

"I'm free, then?" I asked.

"Yes, Andrew, absolutely free."

"Phew!" I exclaimed and fanned my brow.

Dr Murray told me I would need to return to the hospital at some time, just to have a last scan to check everything out. She was sure, however, this would be the end of the saga, and after that, "I was never to darken their doors again."

It took us a little while to actually get used to this news. In a way we still are getting used to it. I keep up most of what I learned. I have yet to have the last scan. I think we both look at life from a different viewpoint now.

All the very best to you, and keep well. Andrew.

Pee Ess: I am still taking the 'GREENS'.

Photo courtesy of Gunnie Moberg

50 Letter from France

'Beaugency'

'We were led along old tiled sloping floors and a row of dark oak doors to the end of the passage where 'our' room was. It was still monastic in its looks, white walls, no paintings, no crucifix thankfully...'

We left ORKNEY on a beautiful early January morning and had a fine drive to Inverness; surprised to see gorse bushes breaking out in bloom. Inverness to Aberdeen (for Andrew's second scan, horrid horizontal stuff and worse), and the following day to Edinburgh. Usual lovely stay with friends before sailing from Rosyth to Zeebrügge. Rough seas were forecast but the Superfast ferry copes beautifully and we were none the worse.

The drive to our house in the Lot from Belgium requires an ovenight stay and we had a destination in mind. However, south of Orleans, Andrew took the wrong motorway – towards Bordeaux. After some initial sighing and despairing, I had another look at the map whilst the sun was setting in front of us and a full moon appeared behind us. "Not to worry," I said overbearingly, "we take the first exit and there is a small town where we might find a hotel." This was achieved, except he missed the turn off at the roundabout. Well, the next small town on the river Loire was not far away and had a nice name: Beaugency. The moonlight was reflected in the river and we followed the turning towards the beckoning river and suddenly we were in front of the Abbey/Hotel, which looked magnificent.

There was a light in some windows – we stopped for a closer look: Hotel Touristique *** and the faded menu, which was most enticing and rather expensive. Not quite what we had budgeted for, but did we really want to start looking elsewhere in the encroaching darkness? We climbed the grand stone stairway and found a glass door leading to a large foyer. Here we spotted a receptionist who told us the price of a room (again more than we had intended to spend). We rather liked the idea of staying in a monk's cell, albeit in comfort. We were led along old tiled sloping floors and a row of dark oak doors to the end of the passage where 'our' room was. It was still monastic in its looks, white walls, no paintings, no crucifix thankfully, only old dark oak furniture. A 28-paned window flanked by four-metre-high tapestry-inspired curtains looked on to an avenue of plane trees and the Loire with a lovely bridge, that was to lead us on our way the next day. The moon looked straight at us. Dark double doors in our room revealed a very comfortable bathroom – soap and gels smelling of Lilly of the Valley. The only incongruous piece of furniture was a television, which we did not watch anyway.

We bathed and changed in anticipation of our lovely dinner in a large, yet intimate, dining hall with stuffed boar's and stag's heads high up at either end. The huge fireplace burned two-metre-long logs – all for us and a few other guests. The menu did not let us down – everything was done to perfection and the local wine, Saumur, was excellent, if a bit pricey. Andrew said I looked happy despite the extravagance, which was not going to spoil it for us.

Next morning we wanted to see the actual Abbey, which turned out to be magnificent with wonderfully carved capitals on solid pillars – a Roman apse with a sunken area and sunlight reflecting the stained glass windows on the pale grey stonework.

Strolling on, we came upon the Saturday market – everything as good, if not better, than our Gourdon market. What a piece of luck: we purchased vegetables, oysters, a rabbit, some chicken livers, resisting the temptation of the plump-breasted pigeons – and more and more. We found a lively café and had our much needed coffee and croissants, not having had breakfast at the hotel. The atmosphere so jovial and no ban on smoking – as it should be as far as I'm concerned – or it would not be France. Again I was happy.

We reached Tourriol by detours (voluntarily) early evening – met by our neighbours, pleased to see Andrew well. We inspected the garden, then entered – a very cold house that had not been lived in since summer. Little by little we warmed up are now catching up with friends and planning our stay till early April.

Sigrid

51 Letter from France

'The truffle outing'

*'We were almost knocked back by the odour; one can hardly
call it perfume, more animal-like than other fungi smell.'*

This year we decided to go to the truffle market in Lalbanque, south of Cahors, where only the true Black Perigord specimens are sold. In fact, this is the weekly market on a Tuesday afternoon during January, February and March. We arrived just in time for lunch, so we thought, but every table in the two restaurants were taken. We entered a third place where people were seated at long tables in a convivial manner, but it turned out to be 'members only'. It was the headquarters of the Syndicate for Perigord Truffles, not for us to join in. We re-traced our steps to the more modest of the two restaurants, having been told that we would not be served lunch until their second sitting at 2pm at the Lion D'Or. There we placed ourselves at the bar – at least we could have a drink and wait in hope. After half an hour, one small table was vacated and we cheered up. The waitresses were run off their feet serving such a crowd, and the kitchen had run out of hens and lemon tarts, but we got a steak instead, and apple tart – five courses in fact: soup, chacuterie, main course, cheese, and dessert, all for 12 euro including a quarter carafe of wine per person and coffee. How do they do it?

By 13.30hrs, the sellers started walking slowly up the long street, aptly called Avenue Les Truffes, carrying their little baskets containing their recent harvest of truffles, wrapped in gingham cloth. They took up their positions behind long trestle tables, that were cordoned off until the sale started at 14.30hrs.

Buyers, visitors, tourists, including some Japanese, thronged the street. Some had brought their cute looking truffle hounds; the men mostly wearing flat caps, but we spotted several elegant Astrakhan hats, furs and cigars. It was a very cold, raw February afternoon.

An inspector in camel coat and hat rushed around in front of the cordon with paper and pencil, deciding the value of each 'catch'. As truffles have been scarce the last few years, the prices have become quite silly. This year the top price was 1,000 euros per kilo!

At 14.30hrs sharp, a whistle blew equally sharply and the sale began. It was a frenzy: I have never witnessed any sale take such a short time – all over in ten minutes, apart from one youngish man, looking more like a poet than a farmer, who was left with his lot, but eventually sold them singly, or in small amounts. Otherwise a vendor normally sells everything in one lot and he then covers his truffles in the cloth, no more prodding and sniffing from the public.

Andrew took lots of photographs with his new digital camera; he calls it Fraser – don't ask me why.

One buyer and his expensive-looking wife, apparently bought SEVEN kilos; they were in the foyer of the Mairie (The Town House) writing cheques, well, Madame did, and he, obviously delighted with his purchase, kindly let us have a whiff of his truffles held in two large carrier bags. We were almost knocked back by the odour; one can hardly call it perfume, more animal-like than other fungi smell. He would be supplying hotels and restaurants in Paris, or wherever, and no doubt make a handsome profit.

Apart from where such large amounts of money are concerned, sales are conducted in cash only. Many a Franc note must have found its way under the mattress, including our neighbour's. He confided that he had found 300 grammes of truffles this winter, but I doubt he made 300 euro.

A day to remember.

Sigrid

James D Rowan – as Noel Coward

Andrew's family: Uncle Jerry, Brother Malcolm,
'The Old Man', Daisy Beetroot, Mum (Madge), Brother Stuart.
Andrew took the photo.